CORPORATE TURNAROUND
GLOBAL PERSPECTIVE

Dr Michael Teng

Published in 2008 by
Corporate Turnaround Centre Pte Ltd.

Printed in Singapore
by Markono Print Media Pte Ltd.

9 8 7 6 5 4 3
09

ISBN   978-981-08-0881-5

CORPORATE TURNAROUND: GLOBAL PERSPECTIVE

Table of contents

CHAPTER ONE—.Turnaround Consideration

Chapter Topics

CHAPTER TWO—Guidelines to consider for the turnaround phase

Chapter Topics

CHAPTER THREE—Stabilizing for change

Chapter Topics

CHAPTER FOUR—The product defines the company

Chapter Topics

CHAPTER FIVE—The turnaround options

Chapter topics

CHAPTER SIX—Accounting and financial considerations

Chapter topics

CHAPTER SEVEN—International Trade Considerations.

Chapter Topics

iv

Background of the Author

Dr. Mike Teng is the author of a best-selling book "Corporate Turnaround: Nursing a sick company back to health," in 2002 which is also translated into the Bahasa Indonesia. In 2006, he authored another book entitled, "Corporate Wellness: 101 Principles in Turnaround and Transformation." He also published in 2007/2008 five management books, namely entitled: "Internet Turnaround: The Use of Internet Marketing to Turnaround Companies;" "Training Manual: Corporate Turnaround and Transformation Methodology;" "Link Baiting to Improve Your Page Ranking on Search Engines" and "Corporate Turnaround: Global Perspective as well as Fundamentals of Buying and Selling of Companies."

Dr. Teng is currently the Managing Director of Corporate Turnaround Centre Pte, Ltd. which provides corporate training and management advisory services. He has 28 years of experience in corporate turnaround, strategic planning and operational management responsibilities in the Asia Pacific. Of these, he held Chief Executive Officer's positions for 18 years in multi-national and publicly listed companies.

Dr. Teng served as the Executive Council member for fourteen years and the last four years as the President of the Marketing Institute of Singapore (2000 – 2004), the national marketing association. Dr. Teng holds a Doctor in Business Administration (DBA) from the University of South Australia, Master in Business Administration (MBA) and Bachelor in Mechanical Engineering (BEng) from the National University of Singapore. He is also a Professional Engineer (P Eng, Singapore), Chartered Engineer (C Eng, UK) and Fellow Member of several prestigious professional institutes namely, Chartered Institute of Marketing (FCIM), Chartered Management Institute (FCMI), Institute of Mechanical Engineers (FIMechE), Marketing Institute of Singapore (FMIS), Institute of Electrical Engineers (FIEE) and Senior Member of Singapore Computer Society (SMSCS).

CORPORATE TURNAROUND : GLOBAL PERSPECTIVE

Chapter Topics

- **Introduction**
- **Definition of terms**
- **A struggling company in the world marketplace**
  1. The stockholders of the struggling company
  2. A proper and early diagnosis is the foundation for rescue and recovery
  3. The key to prevention is anticipation
  4. Management and mimicritis
  5. The roles of the CEO, board of directors, and shareholders when a company is sick.
  6. Corporate structural barriers.
  7. Understanding the term turnaround

Out of Clutter, find simplicity
From discord, find harmony
In the middle of difficulty, lies opportunity.
--Albert Einstein

INTRODUCTION

This book is written to help readers understand that there is a path that leads out of the woods of corporate disaster by implementing certain essentials of corporate turnarounds. The tools may vary from country to country, but the general turnaround principles are similar. As in the world of medicine, certain symptoms may look alike; however, the treatment must be appropriate to the patient, the culture, and the diagnosis. As George Bernard Shaw, the famous British playwright once stated: "The only absolute is there are none." This book provides a number of remedies and resources to bring the company, or we should say the patient, back to health, or keeping a healthy company well.

Business plays an important role in the global marketplace and society, but it can only fulfill this role in cooperation with others such as the public sector, labor, and proper environmental practices. When a company struggles in a turnaround phase, it is faced with saving itself—self-survival—may be it will be difficult to collaborate with other sectors, but it is essential to do so. The partnership approach is often the trail through the

woods that can save a lost company. But it may take an experienced pathfinder to show the way. Step one in all troubled company cases calls for action not rhetoric, and the earlier the diagnosis is reached and a treatment plan implemented—the quicker the patient will recover. Although it is the creator of a corporation, the law does not bless it with immunity to sickness just like any human being. As a result, the medical and wellness world is being taken into reference in this book to describe, compare, and examine the essentials of the turnaround process.

There are many stockholders in a corporate turnaround. Stockholders are often missed in assessing the diagnosis and treatment for the turnaround plan in a sick company. These stockholders, for example, do include the shareholders, company core assets, such as good and creative employees, loyal customers, financial backers, and in some cases the general welfare of a community—in other words—people. Later in this book we will describe these as assets that do not show on a company's books, but are essential in a company's health, growth, or recovery.

Generally there are three treatment plans for a company that requires change:

- rescue,

- work out, and

- recovery or liquidation.

Note: maybe to give some definition or an example of rescue and specifics in recovery or liquidation would be more appropriate in this book too.

Work outs are the normal course to bring companies back to health throughout Asia. It has often been mentioned that the Confucian ethic of harmony in conjunction with the desire to "save face" creates an environment where the company and its management avoid liquidation except in severe cases. This is not the case in the U.S. and some western countries where bankruptcy is part of the sick company's early treatment plan. A balance of turnaround options between the West and the East seems desirable in the consideration of stockholders in a company. Transparency, responsibility, and laws that respect the complexities of corporate governance that the people and the companies trust are the goals. In this regard, treatises and other knowledgeable sources in both the East and the West cite Singapore as an example of East and West balance.

Likewise in health, what is good for the sick person may also be good for the healthy person: no one can argue against preventive care for people or companies. Many medical programs today reward a healthy practice of diet, exercise, and thought. A great deal is saved in preventive action and investment. Companies are like people in that regard.

What makes a recovery successful can also be the same preventive medicine, practice, and therapy that sparks up a healthy company. The turnaround tools discussed are useful either way.

In a turnaround, all stockholders may consider they are equal, but find out that some will be more equal than others.[1] It is imaginable that a CEO or the board can be too early in asking for help when the temperature rises, the blood pressure increases, and the hemoglobin drops to single digits, but that is not usually the case. In most company crisis, the specialist doctor is called in too late. Hospital beds are filled with patients who never get themselves treated before their sickness became worse. Meanwhile, the courts are crowded with cases where parties are chasing after the last remaining blood in a company's body. It has been mentioned that experience is a good teacher; however, most of us prefer to learn by someone else's experience. The past can be a different planet in this fast-moving global marketplace, or a source of lessons that a company overlooks at its peril. We will look at the different perspectives of companies from all sizes and ways to keep our companies healthy.

Global companies whether well or sick are facing new challenges: currency valuations, trade barriers, labor and the environmental concerns, tax structures, agricultural and industrial subsidies, trade alliances, inspections, and rogue disorder, natural disorders, intellectual property laws, trade barriers, and the Internet..

---

[1] *Animal Farm*, by George Orwell, 1974

4

Although this writing is useful for managers, business students, investors, and others dealing with both large or small companies and listed or private companies—doing business either domestically or globally—the major emphasis will be placed on listed and global companies, but in many turnaround cases, whether the company be large or small, the tools of turnaround apply to all.

Definition of terms :

Turnaround: A process of restoring, improving or maintaining a company's health.

Mimicritis: In a turnaround situation, before a proper diagnosis is reached, doing of what others do or blindly following popular pressures.

Reasonable care: The standard of care a prudent person uses in his most important decisions.

Trustee care: Trustee care is care that is the highest degree of care.

Bankruptcy: A last resort. A governmentally-judicial process where the judge is the CEO, company control is handed over to the court. Its major goal is restructuring and turnaround under the protection of the court. It can be voluntary or involuntary. Bankruptcy is a very expensive process where the assets of the company are used to pay for attorneys, court costs, and trustees. It can be a savior or a killer of the business. Shareholders most generally lose their investment in bankruptcy. In the business world of today, bankruptcy and liquidation are both used to describe a company in a critical care phase.

Retrenchment: This is a time for a sick company, calling for a strong emphasis on cost and asset reductions to reduce the conditions responsible for a financial downturn. The two objectives of the retrenchment for a company are a return to a positive cash flow and survival. This stage precedes the recovery stage of a turnaround. It is accomplished by such actions for example as: head count cuts, product elimination, and divestment, partial liquidation, managerial changes, improvement of operational efficiency. It is planned as a short term remedy,

Recovery: The time following the entrenchment or overlapping with the retrenchment involves new managerial moves, new markets, improved products, possibly new leadership, and closely monitored finances with higher communication internally in the company.

Leadership: The most important element in the turnaround process.

Letter of Credit: A document issued by an approved bank to the seller from funds set aside by the bank from the buyer and guaranteed payable to the seller upon the fulfillment of certain conditions, such as delivery, installation, and performance. This has been being widely used in the turnarounds and international transactions and in large construction projects. Document should be irrevocable, and in an agreed form of currency as to amount and date. A major credit improvement above a simple account receivable, as it can be used as collateral for the cost of goods to build or provide.

Restructuring: The strategic process in the realignment internally by changing macro environmental factors.

A Developing Company Struggling in the Business World

1. The stockholders of the struggling company.

Companies, small and large in all regions of the world, are susceptible to change—it is only common sense. It is like our health. We are well—then we are not so well. We meet with accidents and sicknesses that seem to strike faster than the causes or symptoms. Then we must recover. A corporation must begin a turnaround before the situation grows worse. What happens during this turnaround process, and who are the stockholders? Why did this happen? The "Why?" may or may not be agreed upon completely at first or even someday later—but first the bleeding must be stopped.

The owners of the public listed company are the shareholders—they are the landlords—even though absentee landlords. The good employees are often the heart of the company. In a corporate class recently, a professor drew an upside down triangle with the base on the top. In the professor's opinion the customers should be on top of any organizational chart followed by the good employees, and then the shareholders. The point, or in this case the bottom, was reserved for management. Perhaps this is a little too lopsided a picture, but it illustrates a truth that cannot be overlooked.

A company is a mosaic with people and forces as its parts. The board of directors is granted the trust to establish the management of the company by the shareholders. They are responsible to assure the company remains in good health. They are the bosses that choose the CEO, who is in charged of managing the company, in the interest of the shareholders—and they must keep the company profitable and out of the negative media and financial graveyards. This mosaic operates within the web of a community of people, institutions, culture, politics, economy, and laws. It is no pile of isolated rocks in the Pacific; it has its corporate rights in most countries of the developed world. So, it is not an easy task to determine a company's recovery path, which may or may not change, with all these stockholders. In a good season it might be easier, but when the creditors and customers are complaining, it is a difficult challenge. We go to experts for help with our illnesses. A struggling company is no different, it requires an experienced professional

The stockholders are the shadow behind every decision whether the company is a manufacturer or a service provider. In a way, the product or service is a stockholder also. Forgetting the product and service that had been distracted by the financial numbers has put many a CEO on a bus heading only one way: out of town. The health of the product and the service may have a major impact on improving the company health. Dell Computers is one company that has grown and succeeded by using experts to make their product healthy. When they moved into the printer business they did so with their usual clean-and-fast mindset. Instead of investing in expensive factories and hard assets that are inflexible assets, or funding an expensive new design team, they relied upon experienced experts and allied with them: Fuji Xerox and Samsung for laser printers, and Lexmark for inkjet printers, and Kodak for digital photo-printing technology.

Ford Motor Company in 2006 was hit by at least two major torpedoes, Toyota, and an over-inventory of fuel thirsty products, which resulted in huge losses in 2006. To their credit, they moved decisively.

Ford's family member CEO understood that the dilemma facing the company, and that it was too much for him to solve. Ford decided upon a non-family member as CEO. They borrowed from banks when they still could for the tough times ahead. They retained a turnaround team from outside the company. The board's swift action that was well communicated to their shareholders, employees, and customers was understood and accepted by the shareholders with hardly a fluctuation in the listed share prices. They were wise enough to know that they needed professional and experienced doctors for their survival.

Before the board of directors purchases the bus ticket for the CEO, they must consider one of the turnaround options, that of seeking expertise in all realms. One of the worst mistakes that management often makes is to try and solve the problem from the inside, similar to self-diagnosis after a sick person reads the latest "How-To" book on self-treatment. Action, not reading is needed along with a good dose of external turnaround expertise.

2. **A proper and early diagnosis is the foundation of rescue and recovery**.

Like in health, self-diagnosis is dangerous and best avoided. Self-diagnosis and treatment provides a good business for bankruptcy lawyers and undertakers.

 Let's call him Kin: Kin was a CEO of a fine company. He used experts that were experienced, capable, and trusted to help him keep his company healthy.

But he was not feeling well. At his last physical examination, his liver tested in the questionable range.

He was not a drinker, was careful in taking his multi-vitamins daily, and even the fact that he was 60, he still played a tough game of tennis. He read all the details he can get on how to make his liver recover: drinking dandelion tea, tomatoes, eating more liver, which was one of his favorite foods, and no more alcohol. He took more vitamins, resulting to abrupt increase of his iron levels; in fact his iron level was quite shockingly remarkable. His wife and the corporate board members urged him to seek an expert at the Mayo Clinic, a famed clinic for difficult cases and diseases.

What he found out through the help of a world-renowned physician was that he was in a state of shock. What he was doing to treat himself was suicide. He was killing himself through his own mouth. His body overproduced iron, and like filings of steel this overproduction attacked his organs and began destroying them over time. To make it worse and a fatal condition, the usual harmless daily multi-vitamin's iron load was a huge mistake. His liver was irreparable—it was too far gone to ever work normally again. He learned that the liver is essential to almost everything in his total body. He now faced a certain death. The diagnosis was that he had the genetic condition of hemochromatitis. This is an inherited condition, mainly running in European blood lines is largely undiagnosed or misdiagnosed, and millions die from this silent killer every year. But he now knew what the cause of his death would be.

Through the human kindness of a cyclist who was killed on his motorcycle, and who donated his organs for helping others, Kin received a transplant: a life and death turnaround. Kin is a thankful and smiling CEO again.

What a struggling company often needs is what Kin needed. Without the expert's eyes, ears, and training he would have died undiagnosed or the guesses would all have been wrong. His self-care was commendable, and in no way does Kin's case oppose self-care: He would have died much earlier, or missed becoming an acceptable transplant candidate, if he hadn't taken good care of himself in controllable areas by keeping fit and informed.

We move down a decision tree in making a correct diagnosis of a company's health. Due to major problems, some companies are sick. In surgery there are times when the patient has reached the end, the diagnosis has been made, the cutting stopped, and hopefully the patient will have some time to reflect on his life with pain monitoring before saying goodbye.

Change management must prioritize its steps carefully and make sure they have made a clear and accurate picture of the patient, the company's ailments, otherwise several years could be wasted and the patient made worse or untreatable. Repeated needs for surgery are bad omens Very soon, surgical help cannot be given because the patient is physically too weak to handle another surgery.

Focusing the turnaround management with change capital may be the best bang for the buck and the weakening of company's best medicine. This often instills confidence of change for the company, its employees and shareholders (The Ford example). The patient that holds hope will always do better. The diagnostic approach is good for more than once: it needs to be institutionalized for the company to handle changes in the future. It is part of the recovery.

3. **The key to prevention is anticipation.**

Preventing a downturn requires a proper diagnosis of the reasons and then action. The remedial action can come in many forms that are covered in this text. Although mergers, acquisitions, and alliances may distract the CEO and management from solving the sickness of the company, there are examples of carefully planned alliances with the assistance of experienced and professional experts that have been successful in saving a company. This has been particularly true in Asia. Alliances, whatever form they take, seem to work better in cultures that are used to working together in teams, such as many of the Asian and Asian/Pacific countries.

Alliances can be a helpful vaccination for a company if administered soon enough. Hopefully, it can prevent the need for stronger anti-biotics later. An example is the Samsung-Mitsubishi alliance that began in 2001, allowing both companies to develop new products quickly by fusing their expertise in design and product development. They retained their independence with separate product releases. They didn't risk financial resources and brand identity in buying each other out.

In another example, there was a need of action before Dell and Minco were lost in the dust of competition. They are examples of what companies must consider, as people do with regular exercise to stay healthy and competitive, because "turnaround" should be a daily component of growth not decay. These two companies turned around their way of doing business. Dell for example, moved out of the manufacturing business and became in essence a general contractor, sub-contracting its products to other companies to manufacture. It concentrated on a direct sales approach to customers throughout the world that was greatly helped by an early and strategically planned internet marketing program.

The middle-sized company of Minco from the middle of the US is in a highly competitive business of medical and aeronautical technology and found that they could not meet their customer needs. Many of their customers were in the Asia/Pacific market area and demands were made for customization of their product they could not provide. Loss of sales and profits were at stake—and worse—the loss of a faithful customer base in Asia/Pacific. In June of 2006, under expert advice, they researched the best country in the Asia/Pacific market area for them to quickly establish a design and service center. Because of Singapore's record for smooth corporate operations, such as the ability to exchange currencies freely, and the nation's considerable medical and aeronautical technology resources, they chose Singapore. Instead of lost sales they are now reporting increased sales (www.minco.com).

When the stockholders and the company need revitalization due to low profits, high losses, and low sales—these are some of the many reasons a turnaround is needed--the slope of operation and recovery can become rather slippery. The price of waiting too late is high. For example, the CEO and the board at VNU, the Dutch media company, decided the company could make itself better by making an acquisition. The largest shareholders of VNU strongly objected to the huge cash outflow it would take--throwing the company into one of Europe's fiercest corporate battles.

The acquisition was halted, but rather than returning the money to the shareholders and the company, VNU's management jumped to another acquisition--either rightly or wrongly. VNU's shareholders under its by-laws and articles had the *right to vote* on acquisitions. The shareholders forced the management to abandon this second acquisition. The board then agreed to sell all of VNU to a group of private equity firms. However, that became unpopular, too. The shareholders forced the buyers to raise their takeover price even more than the board had agreed to as the selling value of the company. Needless to say, the trust between the management and the stockholders was caput by then.[2]

While the shareholders may own the company, MOST corporations DO NOT state in their charters and by-laws that the shareholders have a vote on the company's major decisions such as mergers and acquisitions as was in the VNU charter. Whether it's good or bad that shareholders have a vote depends on the shape of the company mosaic. The VNU case management claimed that the shareholders were overly aggressive. Such aggression can blow a good chance at recovery or turnaround, or it can save the company a major financial burial. But CEO, board member, or shareholder, each should know what the company's Articles and By-laws say about shareholder rights and prepare accordingly.

---

[2] *Wall Street Journal, PA3 4 November 2006*

4. Management and *mimicritis* (A jerky reaction to what others do).

Think three times before
Taking any action—Confucius

In most troubled companies, the doctor is called in too late. Hospital beds and bankruptcy courts are filled with those of us who never got around to taking care of something before it became worse: This is true in turnarounds.

So who should do the request for help? Ever notice who a newly elected official chooses for cabinet? Those people that are known and trusted. Will they be objective? Some will and some won't. In a turnaround situation both objectivity and trust are needed plus competency. In many cases a turnaround will fail unless external expertise is sought.

Most CEOs should know or plan who they should ask in the boat to help row when the sails are taken over by the wind. Of course, like death, we prefer to believe that it's someone else's problem. It will never happen here. But in just one western country alone (USA), over 2000 companies applied for bankruptcy relief for restructuring and turnaround assistance in the last two years.[3] Compared with China, for example, although modern laws exist, it was rarely used, and of the 200,000 businesses in China it is estimated that fewer than 2,000 bankruptcy cases have been resolved by the courts in the last eight years.

Services of accountants, lawyers and analysts are needed by management in forming a support and planning team. However, as we saw in the VNU case the shareholders must not only be informed, but also communicated with them as much as possible. Planning

---

[3] *US Bankruptcy Court statistics, 2005*

17

groups and boards have a history of following a phobia of *mimicritis*—the tendency to get in step and do what others have done. This usually results in terminating the CEO with a big splash in the media. Maybe this will let everyone off the hook and keep the stock steady for a while: some times a very short while! They are following an Old Russian saying of "A fish rots from the head, until the head falls the rot will spread."

The lawyer sees it as a legal problem—the accounting firm as a numbers failure—the banker often looks through the wrong end of the money glass. What are really needed in a planning team are members who are first of all people with vision, trustworthiness, experience, and innovation. But often the crisis is one that none of the members has been through before. They need an expert as a patient needs a doctor.

Then, secondly the people on whom the company depends upon for assistance and growth must have traits and experience that give them certain needed competencies. It is often this team that decides to bring in an experienced turnaround professional: someone from the outside—someone from the front lines when a turnaround is needed—the turnaround expert.

The turnaround expert who handled one of the largest cases of corporate trouble in the last decade, Enron Energy Company, found the huge multi-national energy company was comprised over 2000 companies—an absolute maze of corporate intestines. The expert performed the work first of all as a skilled investigator hampered by the state of the company: many of the principals of company management would not help or talk because they were under criminal indictment charges for fraud. The turnaround firm found these subsidiaries and companies in Asia, Europe, the Americas, and Africa.

The new turnaround team decided that the first priority was to sort out all these companies. Since the company was in bankruptcy at the time (2001), there was considerable pressure to sell all the hard assets of the company immediately, such as the pipelines, by the creditors who were understandably nervous as they were owed billions of US dollars. The turnaround team resisted.

As it turned out, the case of this multi-billion dollar company was resolved rather quickly when others of a lesser nature would take many years in court. The court is considering a bonus payment to the turnaround expert team that made the right decision. Today, Enron is still in business with some of the hard assets (including the pipelines) paying creditors and hiring workers back—headed by a new and highly principled management.[4]

In the Enron case the CEO was terminated immediately when the discovery of fraudulent transactions and back-dating of stock options were discovered, but in other cases a number of CEOs claim that they are wrongfully accused of the company's weakening position, and claim they have been prematurely terminated when patience would have corrected the shaky course of the ship. What shoved Enron from millions to billions in losses was the management's concealments rather than dealing with the problems as they came along and taken action when needed. It is always easier to hide or try and buy success than do the grubby work of a turnaround—a short sighted solution. Enron's intricate and fraudulent system will be examined later in this book.

---

[4] *Break From The Pack,* Oren Harari, Financial Times Press, 2007

5. The roles of the CEO, board of directors, and shareholders

Four Seasons Hotels: Although the following case is not a turnaround situation, it is like certain turnaround cases where shareholders receive their news from the media and not from their trusted money-holders, such as the CEO and the board of the company where they often have invested their pensions and life savings. In a recent case involving the Four Seasons Hotel chain, Canada, the owner of the four star Singapore Four Seasons, and many others throughout the world, an offer to buy the company was made--then accepted by the CEO and board of Four Seasons and the shareholders had no right of vote to oppose it. The new offer was lower than what was earlier offered by another prospective buyer that was rejected by the CEO. The earlier bid would have given the shareholders a higher price for their shares, but this later bid gave the CEO special benefits. The shareholders had little influence and the lower priced deal was accepted by the CEO and the board.[5]

Should the shareholders have rights to vote on the destiny of their fortunes? Since mergers and acquisitions can save or ruin a company, and it's one of the turnaround options—many argue they should have. There are many reasons, such as in the Four Seasons case, where price is not everything, and in view of the buyers: Cascade Investments—Bill Gates (Microsoft) and Kingdom Hotels—Prince Walid bin Tatal of Saudi Arabia, there is a good basis to believe the acquisition will turn out well for the shareholders and the CEO. However, that is not often the case.[6]

---

[5] *"Chief of Four Seasons Hotels Makes Buyout Proposition,"* The New York Times, 7 November 2006
[6] Four Seasons, supra.

Just as adrenalin acts to the human, talk of takeovers, mergers and acquisitions can push shares up in the beginning and often fooling those who need to know. In a November 2006 article by *Bloomberg Business News* the headline was: "Talk of Takeovers Pushes Asian Shares Up." Certain records were set in the stock index in Hong Kong and in the Straits Times index in Singapore.

This bump in stock values when talk of mergers and acquisitions hit the media and raised a *multi-national media company* shares in the beginning. But the health of the company soon faltered as the shareholders of the company lost confidence in management. Since in most corporations, the shareholders have no right to vote on management decisions—major or minor—the shareholder role is often misunderstood, and they are neglected by management as management (CEO and the board) and often choke in the maze of numbers and financial threats to the company. While shareholder rights cases have increased in the last decade in most court systems, in absence of fraud by management, they have largely been unsuccessful. As stated earlier, in most company Articles and By-laws—few or no rights of review over management decisions exists and the laws reluctantly intrude in this free market and governance area.

But an overly aggressive group of shareholders can doom a company, tying it up in a whirl of lawsuits and disharmony when a turnaround is needed. Shareholders have also created situations that have caused a downfall in the company and the need of a turnaround by demanding dividends and growth when it is not supported by the numbers and cash flow. One CEO complained that he never slept at the end of each quarter—the pressure was always there to improve earnings. It is clear that a proper balance is needed between the shareholders and management all throughout and not just on turnaround or in time of trouble—communication is always critical.[7]

An example of poor communication and civil war occurred in a media company case where the stockholders had enough of low earnings. They organized and insisted that the CEO must go—without any specific reason other than the company's low earnings. The earnings for the entire newspaper industry were also lowered. Low earnings meant low stock prices, and the shareholder's fears of losing their investment prompted them to take action. The board terminated the CEO and hired a new CEO (2004), who made the usual front-end smash of selling off an asset of the company. It was unfortunately one of the assets of the company that was the most profitable, a newspaper in London. Two years later, with profits lowering again and most of the cash from the sale gone from the sale of its prime jewel, the second CEO slipped into trouble with the stockholders--and management is again considering as a turnaround option—sale. The former CEO is now also suing the company claiming over-zealous stockholders pushed it into trouble.

---

[7] "Chicago Sun Times," in New York Times, 1 November 2006

6. **Corporate structural barriers.**

In reviewing the roles of the parties in a corporate structure, while it is true the board of directors are not a trustee owing a fiduciary capacity to the shareholders in most countries they, however, must use *reasonable care* in their duties as members of the board. They owe this duty to the shareholders. The same goes for the CEO. The shareholders also owe *reasonable* care to their corporation or they can be sued if they damage the company, but this type of lawsuit is rare. It would be like committing suicide or sabotage. By contract or law, the CEO, the board, and the company may also owe other duties to third parties including governmental units.

Reasonable care has been generally defined to mean the care a prudent person would use on his own in very important matters. As long as management (CEO, Board, and Management Consultants) follow their duties of reasonable care, the laws of their jurisdiction, and stay within the scope of their authority according to the corporate Articles and By-laws, they are normally shielded from third party liability. The management of a corporation is different from the historical partnership where in a partnership one partner may be liable for the acts of the other partner or partners. Of course, there are exceptions to these rules and laws depending upon jurisdiction and circumstances.

There has in recent years been an increase of attendance and participation at shareholder meetings in an attempt by shareholders to review or question the direction of *their* company. But there is a barrier at such meetings, and that barrier is the shareholders may voice disapproval, and they may vote on who the Board should be, but they are generally limited in any management rights or changes. These barriers are built into the rules of the corporation by management and can generally only be changed upon a majority-plus vote by the stockholders. The argument is that these barriers are not barriers, but are protections against reactive decisions that are often short-sighted and harmful in the long run to the company.

On the other hand, if one drew an organizational plan under the traditional corporate triangle, at the top would be the CEO and the Board. The employees, customers, and stockholders would be sharing the bottom positions. This has been argued as a barrier position and in fact the triangle should be changed: The customers should be on top, followed by the shareholders.

In the arena of corporate turnarounds these barriers and considerations can aid or hamper the turnaround. These barriers can be overcome if the separatism that is innate in a corporation is trumped by good communication between the levels.

British Petroleum: In August of 2006 a major oil spill occurred in the largest oil producing area of North America. At the same time the price of petroleum had reached a record high on the world market and prices for fuel had almost doubled in some areas.

24

Bankruptcies shot up, and airline flights were limited because of high energy costs. It was a bad time to be throwing oil in the ocean. The worldwide press coverage put the company British Petroleum in a bad light. As usual, the common approach was taken and the CEO was removed but not terminated, and all agreed that a turnaround had to occur so this would not happen again. A new CEO was quickly hired and the former CEO moved to a second position in the company at Alaska.

This Prudhoe Bay, Alaska, petroleum operation under the direction of the new CEO instigated an immediate investigation of what went wrong. The findings showed that the spill was caused by careless maintenance operations and management, causing damage. To solve the maintenance and management problem the new CEO decided the causes were internal, and could only be solved by better communication within the company.

The new CEO established a blog site for the employees to discuss how the company could improve its operations, and in addition, retained outside and independent turnaround and environmental experts to determine how to solve the problem.

The result was that BP accomplished the clean up, repair, and implementation of a new safety and engineering program in one-half the time it would normally take and found safety measures they installed that would prevent further spills.[8]

---

[8] *"Age and neglect meet in global oil pipeline,"* International World Herald, 22 August 2006, and New York Times, *"BP Replacing Head of Alaska Operations, 2 November 2006".*

7. A term defined; Turnaround

When we use the term turnaround, we are using it to cover a range of situations from preventive action to major surgery. Yes, this is a wide range, but there is a relationship between the different parts: the symptoms, the diagnosis, and the solution. There are examples in this book of cases where companies were alert to symptoms, made a diagnosis, often with turnaround expert help (the doctors), and solved the problem before it became critical. In all cases "turnaround" is remedial: reviewing and when necessary—changing.

Global airline industry is full of examples of success. In the US, few passengers know whether the airline they are flying on is in bankruptcy or not. However, some are thriving and out-performing their competition. It is because they diagnosed the business condition that could bring them down early enough to do something about it. And whether in bankruptcy or not, have a strategy and plan operating that will turn the company around.

Toyota of Japan is a prime example of a company that is very successful, but is using this successful phase of its operations to change and improve, pushing innovation, and by corporate philosophy it is in a constant alert to change what is needed. "Resting upon laurels" is not permitted at Toyota.

Another example is Singapore Airlines. Those of us who have flown this airline generally never forget it because of the enjoyable experience aboard. The airline aims to appeal to passengers' senses by combining music, fragrance, and employee demeanor to present a cool and impressive image. Such efforts on the part of the company can make a solid difference when competing with low-fare rivals such as Air Asia. Launching itself from the commodity airline is their key. Quality can be service as well as an element of a manufactured product.

CHAPTER TWO—Guidelines to consider for the turnaround phase

Chapter topics

Calling the right specialist doctor—the turnaround expert

1. **Assembling the turnaround team**

2. **Communication with customers, shareholders, employees, and media**

3. **Customer care**

4. **Goals and objectives**

A competent CEO must know the pulse of the company and run the preliminary tests of how sick or well the company is—this is what the CEO is hired to do. Particularly when profits or sales start to slide downward, a watchful eye on the symptoms in their early phases can prevent further deterioration of the company. It is then that perhaps some medication will only be needed, or a change of diet, or more exercise. And we will first examine what can be done in this phase. A diagnosis must be made quickly and most CEOs who have experienced such a downturn favor immediately bringing in a professional turnaround expert, which can be a small investment at the time, but pay for itself many times the investment and what is important—quickly.

Objectivity from the outside with a confidential relationship from an experienced turnaround expert do prevent major surgery later. The CEO and Board have the option of outpatient visits or a long stay in the hospital, which if they wait could look more like a bankruptcy courtroom.

In the cases examined so far, there are several alternatives that companies can do to avoid major surgery by changing with the help of change artists. At this point we are not talking about terminating the CEO unless there are claims of fraud or criminal conduct. Nor are we at this stage suggesting the selling off profitable parts of the company—that's for a later consideration--if at all. Once the smell of the downturn hits the media or the clubroom, the merger and acquisition firms, along with the private equity companies will come running with their solutions. Getting set to make a turnaround is a great factor in success for the company, and the change artists, the turnaround experts. the doctors--are key in getting set.

The turnaround expert will perform a "due diligence" review of the company from a neutral perspective—a very critical need for most companies. They will notice certain points that may not be obvious to the management. An example is a multi-national computer company that has installed their systems in most of the Asia/Pacific major weather bureaus. Because of moderately sliding profits they cut their usual research and development budget in half, reducing it to 3% from their usual 6%. This was a short-sighted solution that their turnaround expert discovered and convinced them to change. They were in a highly competitive industry and a real improvement was necessary for their designs, product development, and services each year to stay competitive. The early diagnosis prevented a collapse further down the line, which would have been inevitable.[9]

---

[9] MBA notes-Zelium International Ltd.

1. Assembling the turnaround team

In the serious business of company diagnosis and change, the turnaround team should include the professional and experienced turnaround expert and those members that speak their mind. There is no room for spoon-fed information. A hand-picked "yes" team by the CEO may or may not be right kind of people. However, the destiny and health of the company is at stake. It is also assumed that the team members whether internal, or most probably external, will be knowledgeable and highly experienced about turnaround operations.

In the Four Seasons Hotel case, as an example, where the company was doing well, they had secured some outstanding offers to sell the company. To give balance to the decision an independent board of directors was installed to review this major decision of the company. And in that case the CEO was the actor in bringing in the independent board.

With lowering profits in the US, Wal-Mart, the largest retailer in North America made a decision to open operations and engineer a major investment in China. This decision was made in 2006; however it was thoroughly examined by a team of growth and turnaround experts, working closely with management for several years. Their team concluded that China would be the next great market, as the US had been. There were various reasons for their lower profits in the US, and the company introduced a new pricing and employee policy program to stop the descent of profits in the US. They opened three fronts, actually, to make the turnaround—they also increased the number of their Latin American operations. And they did this before the company's condition worsened. This is an excellent example of early diagnosis and prevention.

2. Communications with customers, shareholders, employees, and the media.

As many former politicians have written, it is best to be truthful in what is told to the media. The real decision is *what* should be told to the media. The same goes with shareholders, the company owners, and the employees. To reveal too much too soon is foolhardy for the situation may change, but the landed words may never change or be corrected. To promise too much is risky. Depending upon the facts, unless there is genuine agreement on what a particular issue's answer is by the turnaround expert and team, opinions should be avoided, particularly until the turnaround plan is jelled. This is a prime example of where the experienced turnaround expert's counsel is invaluable as they know how to deal with these important parties: the employees, the shareholders, and the media. These parties are important to the turnaround process and wherever it is feasible and wise to do so--their help should be sought.

3. Goals and objectives.

In many cases the first person who sense that there's sickness within the company are the employees. How they react to efforts by the turnaround team to bring health to the company often depends upon how clear the goals and objectives of the turnaround team plan may be. Clarity and regular communication are critical to keeping the employees' shoulders to the wheel of change in a difficult period for the company. Employees need systems and policies to guide their efforts, goals and measures to track their productivity. This must be a priority of the team, which must be more than a management team, but more importantly a *leadership* team. The goals and objectives that seek the employees' help should not wait—they should come early. Waiting too long and hoping for improvement may gain points in an optimistic type of organization, but it is dangerous in business. Communication is critical because it builds confidence in the employees and strengthens interaction with management and customers, which can spark the turnaround success.[10]

---

[10] *Don't Sweat the Small Stuff,* Rusch Publishing, and Zurich, Switzerland.

CHAPTER THREE—Stabilizing For Change for Turnaround

Chapter Topics

1. **Customer care during a downturn**

2. **Keeping the crows and buzzards away**

3. **Legal considerations**

1. Customer care during a downturn

"Stabilizing for change" may sound inconsistent, for change is rarely made if

boundaries for employees or customers become tighter. A tight-fisted and threatening

approach demanding employees work longer hours for less or customers to pay in

advance is usually self-defeating. The object is to invite the customer to join your side

and help while you are not feeling well. Letting them know that the fever is only

temporary is crucial. And that there will be specific rewards for them along the way if

they help you now by paying on time, or increasing orders, or by employees working

harder and more efficiently. An important part of the turnaround team is to establish a

program for customer communication and developing some extra effort, such as more

service or longer warranties (important items that will not immediately influence cash

flow) for customers. To create change the bleeding has to be stopped and then a clear

understanding of what has to be done communicated.

Jack Welch, the successful former CEO of General Electric gives this advice: "To create change, I believe in the Crotonville/Workout concept: Direct, personal, two-way communication is what seems to make the difference. Exposing people without the protection of title or position, to ideas from everywhere, and judging the ideas on the merits."[11]

[11] *Control Your Destiny Or Someone Else Will*, Jack Welch. Bantam-Doubleday, 1993.

2. Keeping the crows and buzzards away

The limping person is closely watched by eyes unseen, the scalpers, waiting for the right time to pounce. And likewise, the crows have a very sophisticated communication network. A creditor control program needs to be on the charter of the turnaround team.

The creditors are not the only birds to watch: There are the competitors, the buy-out pirates, the fake doctors of business, the private equity hunters, and others.

In a situation where a middle-sized business faced another quarter of losing money the CEO admitted: "The company wasn't there, and the plan just wasn't there and there is no energy driving the company." But from the inside, he was puzzled. He took action and talked to the creditors: "*We* have a choice. We can blow this thing up today, or we can put in a new plan in place that gives this company a chance. I'm not going to pay you for 90 days and that's your best shot in getting your money back." And they agreed.

Under their new plan they reduced overhead and management salaries and brought some new designs into production that had been on the back burner, and narrowed their focus on their core business. The debts have been reduced, the loans current, and the course of losses reversed. [12]

Of course, what works for one company may not work for another. When the company's health is called into question it is the wrong time to figure out whether or not the banks that the company has trusted can still be trusted to work through the downfall.

---

[12] *Lessons From the Edge*, Jana Matthews and Jeff Dennis, Oxford University Press, 2003.

The path taken should be with the counsel of the change or turnaround expert who has been in the ring and understands the consequences of making the wrong judgment. A premature alarm to the company's bank/s can precipitate and worsen the company's health. But in all cases it is the time to make changes while the clock of health still allows for it.

In financing, loans and debts, the earlier they are candidly assessed the better. Refinancing in the early phases of a downturn is still often possible and should be explored. If it's time to change banks—certainly the company should explore that plus other alternatives of change that can prevent further complications. It is a sad statement to make but patients of major illnesses that have recovered have experienced being treated as if they had died during their sickness. People they thought were their friends forgot them quickly. Luckily that is not true with all friends; the loyal ones are there at the end to celebrate with the recovered patient. It is so with companies as well, once the bad news crow starts flying around, valued employees may leave, money becomes tight, and accounts receivable the blood of the company during tough times risk debtors taking advantage of the company's troubles and paying late.

There are a number of different asset protection plans, but they must be utilized early or any transfer is subject to a fraud objection. Before the sickness and the downturn turns serious a company has many options.

3. Legitimacies to Consider

*"The business of business is business. . .but it
ought to be legitimate business and not at
the expense of the future generations."
-Milton Friedman, Economist*

The role of a lawyer differs around the world. In the U.S. a contingent fee program is practised by lawyers who take cases on a percentage of win basis. This is a great help to those without the funds to hire a lawyer for the remedies they are seeking. When the court award is made then the lawyer and the client are paid. If they don't win the lawyer receives only his costs reimbursed, but no fees. If the case is settled before trial the same divisions of money are made. Usually the lawyer earns one-third of the amount that is recovered plus costs. The balance goes to the client.

The U.S. system of "free" lawsuits is highly criticized by others. In most of Europe and Asia this contingent fee system is not allowed. Clients in those continents must have the money to pay for counsel if they want to bring a lawsuit. The contingent fee system is criticized because it encourages claims in great numbers. Many claims sap a company's or individual's resources whether they win or lose. The small aircraft and medium-sized aircraft manufacturers in the U.S. have almost been destroyed by large claims. Most commuter aircraft operating in the U.S are designed and built outside of the U.S. for this reason.

The law is not self-enforcing: it is only a string of words unless there are people to enforce it. The law is like a doctor's medical bag. The medical instruments alone do nothing—how they are used is everything. This is where lawyers come into the picture: they are assigned the duty of giving life to the law. This is a serious and honorable duty. Most lawyers understand this. As in all professions and walks of life some will be untrustworthy and a few will not be. The Enron Energy Company case brought down lawyers, accountants, and executives who defrauded their company, their shareholders, their employees, and their country. Many today are in prison. For those that are not and have been unethical in business they may or may not be able to sleep at night.

Lawyers are not trained in law school as business people, and a legalistic approach to solving a company's struggling problems can be very detrimental. On the other hand, lawyers can be essential and helpful with their experience and training as members of a turnaround team. But people on the turnaround team need to know the difference between selling and marketing, and the difference between treating people as teammates rather than adversaries.

A contract is a negotiable transaction. One of the most important aspects of the contract is the agreement as to the applicable law and jurisdiction in the event of a legal dispute. Ignoring this aspect has thrown a number of companies into a sickness that they often do not recover from. A company from Malaysia might agree to accept the laws of Germany in a contract because it is eager to make a good sale.

The companies that are struggling and in a weakened financial condition are extremely susceptible to making this concession. Even if the German court and law are fair, a case brought in by another country and tried by the court or jury in that other country means major cash out—great expense—win or lose.

Similar to getting into trouble with an out-of-the-country lawsuit, it is taking chances on contract bids such as in the contracting business of building. This happened in Singapore and many sub-contractors were faced with lawsuits in the mid 1990s. The sub-contractors may believe their change orders will be paid even though a provision to do so is not in the contract. And in order to win the contract in the first place they offered to perform the contract with a slim margin. These sub-contractors opened themselves up to general and consequential damages. The big winners were the lawyers.

In another case, a mid-sized computer manufacturer from Japan made its first sale in China to an oil drilling customer in Daijing. The computer company used their new distributor in China to make the sale. One of the most difficult negotiating articles in the contract between the manufacturer and its Chinese distributor was what law would apply. The distributor insisted upon Chinese law not the law of Japan. A compromise was reached to use the law of Hong Kong. When the customer in Daijing paid the distributor the full purchase price of the equipment the distributor kept the money.

After many excuses on what happened to the money, the Japanese computer company which badly needed the sale, filed for their money in Hong Kong Supreme Court. At the trial, the court quickly found ruled against the distributor. It was fortunate that the Japanese computer company chose the Hong Kong legal forum because at the time the Hong Kong decision-making laws and recovery of money laws were far superior to those in China. The computer company would have been headed to the business hospital if this wise decision and plan for their transactions had not been made ahead of time.

Even if a company never does business in other countries all the truths of the terrible cost of litigation apply—only differently—perhaps. In a recent trip from the U.S. to Japan an executive reported that he was greeted in the Tokyo office with a statement he won't forget: "Welcome to the land of production not lawyers," the Tokyo manager proudly announced. In fact, when the contract between the two companies was complete it contained an article calling for both CEOs to meet and confer once a year, privately, to resolve any conflicts or disputes between their companies during the year.

They never had a dispute that reached beyond this agreed practice to the courts.
A person who carries health insurance does not plan for sickness, but like any other kind of insurance it is a great help when needed. Not all countries offer national health insurance, and for some people, the national health system is not their best medical choice for their disease or condition. But when the need arises, it is something that cannot be usually predicted. The same with a company, they will not be able to predict

which customers or third parties will bring a claim or dispute against them. This is why they have to plan ahead to control the controllable factors in business and one of those controllable factors is the type of contract they offer their customers: one that promotes settlement in the event of a dispute. In recent year's arbitration and mediation clauses have been included in many contracts; and they have kept the expense of lawsuits generally within boundaries.

The problem-solving process of mediation and arbitration called for in agreements requires that before any party to the contract can bring a lawsuit; this dispute resolution concept should be the normal part of most contracts or agreements *before* the dispute arises. Both processes must be mutually agreed. The negotiation stage is the time to urge this solution process before the contract is signed. It is often beneficial for both parties.

A struggling company can be killed by a lawsuit, and there will be no turnaround to work out. But if the struggling company has contracts with alternative remedies for solving disputes other than lawsuits, a turnaround is still a real possibility. One sentence can make all the difference.

It is crucial to understand the rules and regulations of the industry your company is competing in. Those rules and regulations may at times be oppressive, but unless legal channels are taken to reverse them, a company must obey them. Understanding them often requires the experience and expertise of someone from the legal profession. To save money without proper professional opinions is like trying save the surgeon's fee by doing your own surgery. Medical and legal advice when needed is a solid investment. A company wastes money and health without such help.

Following the rules and the law is an important step towards company health. If the law is broken the company becomes susceptible to blackmail from competitors and disgruntled employees. A short-term gain may occur from breaking the law, but in the long run lying, cheating, and misrepresenting is like an abandoned dog which often finds his way home to confront his guilty master. There are thousands of years of wisdom about being moral and honest from such great counsels as Moses and Confucius, and others whose wisdom is not dated.

CHAPTER FOUR—The Product Defines The Company

Most new design and product development
comes not from great discoveries,
but from the needs of customers—Jack Welch, GE.

Chapter Topics

1. **Modern Times And Innovation**

2. **Global product and research development—who is the real patient?**

3. **Communication with the distribution network**

4. **Competition and product life analysis**

5. **New Target Markets**

1. Modern Times And Innovation

When the company enters a changed environment it's an excellent time to consider

innovation, which can be an alternative route away from losses. According to a

report by the Innovation Research Centre at the University of Tasmania, Australia,

innovation is not the captive of technology companies, but is clearly a process for

all companies in the design and product development business. In fact technology

companies make up a much smaller percentage of companies in any country than is

usually imagined. In Australia it is about three per cent.

The encouraging point about innovation is that studies have found that the

innovative seed comes not from a particular discovery or invention, but from *what*

customers say they need.[13] Billions of tax dollars are often wasted in trying to shove

innovation into a hole that it won't fit. And as Jack Welch, the former CEO of

---

[13] The Innovation Research Centre, University of Tasmania, in *The Australian*, September (2006).

General Electric contends in his book on change, that too many boundaries in a company can inhibit innovation just at the time it is direly needed.[14]

A turnaround expert was recently named as the CEO of a U.S. sandwich chain named Quiznos. The expert selected was credited with two major successful turnarounds: Burger King a fast-food chain, and Continental Airlines. By using innovative systems he was credited with increasing sales and helping to prepare Burger King for an initial public offering. He accomplished this after only two years as the turnaround CEO of Burger King.

Innovation is the spirit that can be the life saving tonic for a company that's sick. Think of E-mail, antibiotics, television, worldwide banking, FM radios, personal computers, instant and digital cameras, transistorized hearing aids, MRI scanners, artificial insulin, cell phones, synthetic fibers, lasers, not to mention the container shipping that effectively initialized globalization.

The focus used to be on efficiency in global company turnarounds. And efficiency is important at all times. But Google will give you in a search only half as many entries on the subject of CEOs and efficiency as it does for CEOs and innovation. Efficiency used to be the top goal, but it is no longer considered enough in the marketplace. Efficiency and cost-cutting that are associated with it may not be enough today when global competitors can discount you to death.

---

[14] *Control Your Destiny…*, by Jack Welch, supra.

Many global experts believe that a country and a company's future are dependent on breaking innovations. A management process, whether in turnaround or not, cannot overlook why they were doing well in the first place.

On the other hand, there are techniques and operational changes companies take that are described as innovations. But in the turnaround expert's mind they are only techniques of managing an existing business or improving it only at the margins. They may be useful, but have nothing to do fundamentally with innovation change and especially systemic change. Innovation should mean "real change" and not some kind of masked version of change.

2 Global Product Research And Development—Who is the real patient

Just when a company needs innovation in all ways, such as product, design, and customer development--they are short on cash and understandably reluctant to invest in more employees and in a larger Research and Development and Design Department. There is a proven alternative: Cooperative Global Product Development.

As an example of global product development operating as a basic lifesaver for a struggling company, we take the recent decision of both GM and Ford to design and produce smaller autos. Both have lost market share and profits in the North American market and other country and regional markets to Toyota, the largest auto maker in the world, and others. Both GM and Ford have set aside billions of research and development capital to accomplish this restructuring successfully. In both cases, however, they are not new to designing smaller vehicles.

Through collaboration with offshore companies over the years they designed and developed smaller vehicles offshore. In a major switch now, they must bring that accomplished offshore design and development onshore to the US. Because of offshore product design and development they are fighting back against competition by going to the bank and developing what they have to some extent already done—it is not a case of starting over. And the banks as well as the stock market apparently agree. [15]

---

[15] GM and Ford, November 2006, press releases and NYT interviews.

One of the world's most successful companies at design and product development alliances and cooperation with other companies is Toyota from Japan. In the beginning phase, a company may start with a project working on low value products offshore. The goals are usually to reach a lower cost of production, innovation for the product, and also enhance its life cycle. The goal is to stay away from expensive added payroll and bricks and mortar investments in a lean time for the company. A Toyota representative at the Toyota plant in Valenciennes, France, told a reporter from the New York Times in the summer of 2006 that the Toyota French factory, besides bringing on board new designs, would help convince Europeans it is an acceptable product to own and would give Toyota a greater presence in Europe where its sales are starting to grow.

Although the design and production site in Europe is a risk for Toyota, their sales in Europe are climbing as they are in the US, and Toyota according to their manager has for many years had the practice of global design and product development with different factories and companies around the world[16]. With its new "green" vehicles, such as the Toyota Prius, they have a multi-year jump on their competitors because of the innovation they pushed years ago. In so doing they created customers waiting in line to order their new Prius from Toyota all over the world, and in particular the U.S.

---

[16] *Techworld,* November (2006).

—In many countries, including the United States and the European countries, the consumers are demanding the latest in environmental technology.[17] Engineers from such countries as India and China recognize this in their innovations. The demand for the latest in environmental technology means that current products must be redesigned—the global product development team process can be the answer. A newly designed and environmentally advanced data storage product from India that could replace the current storage disks is one example. And all of this is done at lower costs than if it were attempted at the western company's home site. This alone is a crucial factor in turnaround action.

The reason why the alternative of cooperative global design and product development fits so well into the turnaround program of a company is that it conserves financial resources and yet still gives what most companies need in struggling times—a better product.

It is seldom the right time to start building a hospital when the health of the patient is at risk. *So it is with the product, which in many cases of profit downfall is the sickest one* in the company. The process of making the product well cannot wait. Time is often of the essence. However, the process can be less risky but shortened. Most successful western companies seek help in locating the right company in the foreign country to cooperate in their design and product development work. This process is highly recommended as the consulting and resource expert with global experience

---

[17] The New York Times, 29 October 2006. pages B-1, B-8.

knows both ends of the deal and both work cultures. They also know the company's best bet for an ally for good performance based upon their experience and resources.

3 Communication with the distribution network

A struggling company's distribution network is the closest arm of the company to the customer. Without the customer there is no company--no CEO stock options to gripe about or question, or better wages for the company. A company's distribution channel is therefore a major artery in its health. How this channel is treated will determine how quickly the company turns around and whether or not customers will be there when it does. In a recent merger the loyal distributors of company A, operating in the Asia/Pacific region, were not invited to the home office in the US for six months after the merger, although brochures were sent to them of the new product line of company B, the merger partner. Their customers became confused and sales for both company A and company B plummeted in Asia/Pacific.[18]

In the *turnaround plan* for the companies, both were showing a loss at the time of the merger, and communication with the distributor network and customer base was listed as a priority. It is an example of turnaround managers bringing a company back to health by restoring performance and profitability, but the company, like a patient who has received a liver transplant and when released from the hospital, ignores the doctor's orders and goes on a drunken spree. What was gained was blown.

---

[18] MBA notes, Zelium International Ltd. (2005).

4 Competition and product life cycle analysis

Turnaround management's key to recovery, when firms are doing badly, lies in a rigorous review followed by a stabilization program designed to take control, overcome the immediate crisis, and create cash for establishing long term success.

To do this the "due diligence" review by the turnaround experts should include a close examination of the symptoms and causes of decline, the characteristics of crisis situations, and a first draft of a framework for establishing a successful turnaround. An examination of the competition would be included in the analysis.

It may have been some time since the company has concentrated on how its product or service compare against competition, and it may have been some time since the product has been put on the table and objectively examined as to its product life cycle.

One of the advantages of international trade is that a product that has reached the end of its use in one country may be a much needed item in another part of the world. However, international product including services and design life cycles have accelerated substantially. Before, product life cycles could be spread out over a period of several years but now companies must be prepared to face product life cycles that may have lives of only months.[19]

---

[19] *"Product Development the Japanese Way,"* Mossabi Kotabe.

One major issue facing product and design planning will be environmental concerns. Toyota saw it coming ten years ago. Major consumer attention to environmental concerns will be an opportunity for many new products and many new designs, but this factor will also require companies to examine their existing products for compliance or run the risk of governmental or litigation fines and expenses that can be astronomical. There is legislation being considered in both the US and Europe, for example, that will affect any products imported that are not produced in an environmentally safe way, or that fall below minimum standards for environmental performance in the country of import.

Competition may have developed designs and products that can interact with the new ordering systems of larger companies. This may be one market that a struggling company has missed, and will fall back further on unless steps are completed to develop the most current system of marketing and ordering product or service. Ford Motor Company and Microsoft in a joint venture have designed a new ordering system for automobiles. A supplier not fitting into that system will be eliminated. The new factory by Ford in China will have such a system and cooperatively coordinate with the home base system in the US.[20] While the actions of large companies like Ford and countries such as China receive the most headlines, the principles of their problem solving, the DNA of it, can be used by any size company—and in many cases better because the smaller the company—the smaller the bureaucracy—and the faster it can move to solutions.

---

[20] *Trends in International Business,* Michael R. Czinkota and Masaaki Kotabe, (Oxford, England).

Market presence may be necessary to execute certain turnaround strategies. Komatsu of Japan held a market share of 80% in Japan in the heavy equipment industry and moved aggressively in to other country markets. At the time Caterpillar was facing a major labour upheaval in its home plant in the US and its global and domestic sales were in a down-plunge. Its turnaround management strategy called upon it to form a joint venture with Matsushita, Japan to serve the Japanese market. The joint venture has restored Caterpillar to a competitor again and boosted sales also for Matsushita. Sometimes a positive move against competition is necessary. And with a joint venture, the investment is considerably less a drain on the cash flow than most other alternatives.[21]

---

[21] *Partnerships for Profit*, Jordan D. Lewis, New York: Free Press, (1990).

5 New Target Markets

Finding new markets for products and services is the duty of every company sick or healthy on a regular basis. Finding new markets should be allied with other operations of a company and should not be disruptive of core products and services that are producing a positive cash flow. Like consumer service it should not be only the business of the research and development department, but a process for the entire company. It does not take an MBA in marketing to determine that many new areas of sales exist, and in many cases minor modification of objectives, design, and product can focus on a new market in a gradual manner that can be a key to a turnaround or a healthier company. In this regard "going international" or seriously considering it is an important step for a stronger sale.

In many countries today there is an energy challenge together with environmental frontiers that are hungry for solution. The solution can be a product as simple as a solar oven that for example spun one company out of a downward spin of business. Gradually, as the exported ovens to African countries gained sales; these sales were ready when needed to reverse the sales loss of their core business - fish products.

In many countries the only energy resources presently being used are diesel motors and generators. There can be a sky full of products to replace this system for movement and watching television. Just as populations could live longer with the help of antibiotics and other miracle drug, they are dying from the effects of a toxic environment before their time. Huge countries such as the U.S., India, and China will have to invest heavily to lead the way or face huge costs of delay. Polluting today for profit is pirating tomorrow's health.

There are close to 5000 companies in China that sell simple water heater systems for rooftops using solar heat where the water is warmed as it passes through thin pipes crisscrossing a shiny service. It is estimated that this popular use of solar energy is in use by over 30 million households in China. There is a government subsidy to keep the price of the heaters affordable.

According to Mr. Jerry Li with Cleantech China in Beijing, the amount of venture capital money invested with Chinese companies that have turned to environmental products has doubled from the year 2005 to the year 2006. He reported that "Things are changing fast in China. China is looking more intensely at wind, hydro, and solar as alternative and renewable energies." The government has made statements about alternative energies as well, enforcing the program to support companies which renew themselves by changing to producing "green" products so China can be less dependent on oil and imports of oil (Russia). There are more basic products that demand the attention of start-ups and troubled companies, but fall under the loose definition of "green," for example, will meet the demand for potable water and clean food. Mr. Li expects to have a data-base of over 300 Chinese companies in this category seeking investment partners soon in 2007.

The opportunities and the needs of alternative environmental technologies and products can be spun by just a province, a city-nation, or a state without waiting for the nation or world to move. An example is California a state in the U.S. By setting higher standards for energy efficient vehicles, buildings and appliances and requiring power companies to work with customers to reduce consumption of energy, according to the Natural Resources Defense Council, the savings on energy costs has saved California from otherwise having to build 24 giant power plants.

With the increasing number of new companies this change in energy policy has caused difficulty in estimating, but this policy has provided a new market for many companies to change directions.

As these numbers increase the cost of energy and pollution will go down. Wind generators have greatly improved, but are still too costly for many market areas of the world. Some renewable energy plants in India use a common weed to produce a bio-additive to diesel.

The future and current markets for environmental products represent only one often overlooked new or innovation product market area. There are examples of many new market opportunities for companies needing a positive cash flow and growth, and another would be the aerospace and medical fields. The entire medical field is changing by leaps and bounds with new equipment, new systems, and innovative medications. Entire small cities have been built around the production of supplies and services for the medical field.

Many companies have never entered the business of being a governmental supplier, usually the largest buyer in a country. A number of companies have turned around their destinies and returned to health after receiving governmental contracts.

Governmental regulations are now being lifted in some countries allowing a greater number of their governmental purchases to be from any company in any country that is on their authorized list. Some provinces and states provide special categories and give a troubled company priority bid status. The field of business is rich in opportunities that are solid. This section shows only a few examples of minefields of demands for new products.

CHAPTER FIVE—The turnaround options

Chapter topics

1. **The Plan for a turnaround: First phase in turnaround management**
2. **Mergers and Acquisitions and Alliances**
3. **Sack the CEO. Cut payroll. Negotiate with labor**
4. **Other alternative measures or resuscitation**
5. **When Company Faces Problems: Bankruptcy**

1 The Plan for a turnaround: First phase in turnaround management

According to some experts the turnaround plan is the heart of the turnaround

program.[22] In order for the turnaround to work the plan must call for immediate

action within a period of days with goals and objectives clearly agreed to by all

members of the management change team including the change expert. No

turnaround is successful unless the plan *and action program based upon it* is

comprehensive and generates internal cooperation and delivers confidence to the

customers. And the goals of the changed plan must be driven by the change team.

Although the plan must be focused and stable, as Jack Welch, the former CEO from

General Electric Corporation points out, the plan needs to have some flexibility in it

to create an environment of trust, confidence and innovation.

If a wage freeze is decided upon it should be a wage freeze on management as well

as employees, but it should allow for future increases based upon learning and

---

[22] *Corporate Turnaround: How Managers Turn Losers Into Winners. "* Donald Bibeault, Harvard Business School Press, 2001.

improvement. A considerable effort must be made to bring the employees into the fabric of the organization, not just E-mails and handouts now and then, but a new partnership process, such as a patient is given with the support of the patient's caretakers and doctors. It is a time to share power, not secrete it to a few, and to avoid the common top-down syndrome of the corporate structure. Secrets should be kept to a minimum.

These points are emphasized in an excellent book on turnarounds covering the phases of the turnaround process with two hundred cases: *The Harvard Business Review of Turnarounds*, The Harvard University Business School Press (2001).[23] In 2003 Kodak was facing financial disaster. Although its Asian operations were growing, the company was bleeding in the U.S. and Europe from considerable loss of sales to competitors. The investors and creditors put great pressure upon the company. Their position was that this once great imaging company could not make it in the digital world because it started too late, and competition, particularly from Japan who had taken over its market share in core equipment and services. The demand upon management was to use its free cash for dividends and propping up a dying business as much as possible before liquidation or sell-off. The change management team and the CEO developed a different plan and against heave odds stuck to it: They would sell the former cash cow part of the business, such as cameras etc., except in the Asia and Latin American markets--cut the proposed dividends by seventy per cent, and plow US$3 billion into research and development in the digital market. Courage and a clear plan of action saved the

---

[23] *The Harvard Business Review On Turnarounds*, The Harvard Business School Press (2001).

company, and it developed into a major competitor again in the digital world marketplace with considerable performance improvements in growth and profits. The bets are that it sails back from the doldrums.

2 Mergers, Acquisitions and Alliances

A company's turnaround team may decide that their best bet to recovery or in improving the company is by merging with another company or by selling. Australia's largest airline, Qantas Airlines struggled with losses like many other airlines in the world, and in December of 2006 their board voted to sell to a private group or consortium containing companies from Canada, the U.S. and Australia.

And in their case the buyers were not another airline, but a member of the buying team was a former president for British Airways. The price the board approved was actually higher than the market price. Like other countries, Australia has a governmental requirement that no more than 49% of the company can be foreign owned, and that was met in this case. Other significant airline leaders were part of the buying team, including a former Cathay Pacific executive.[24]

After cutting a significant number of employees around the world and narrowly avoiding deadly labor strife and strikes, Northwest Airlines, with many Asia Pacific routes, hired a turnaround expert team. They already decided that their best option is to merge with another airline and therefore increase their efficiency.

---

[24] *Qantas Board Accepts Offer of 11.1 Billion A$ For a Buyout. Sydney, Australia, 14 December 2006*

The result would end in fewer planes, less routes, and higher fares—therefore more profits. It is questionable whether the customers will be happy with this result. And customer satisfaction is always a factor in a merger. Northwest, however, is in bankruptcy, and some of its other options are not available any longer.[25]

The major disadvantage with merger and acquisition phobia by nervous management in a company is it becomes a distraction to what is really making the company sick. With all the publicity that it draws it can be like trying to fix a toothache by several shots of whiskey, producing only short term results that can be deadly in terms of not meeting the problem face to face. A company's health does not usually improve by more complexities of management and operation. The CEO may be off the hook for a while dealing with a merger or acquisition, which means that CEO may not be solving the problems at home. Numerous articles by the Wall Street Journal and the Wharton School of Business indicate that approximately 60% of all mergers and acquisitions fail.

In most mergers of "equal" the buyer – and there is always a buyer – pays little or no premium. Both the companies simple participate in a stock swap on the assumption that the shares will rise because of the cost savings and "synergies" (A dynamic state in which combined action is favoured over the sum of individual components action).

---

[25] *New York Times, 14 December 2006 (Northwest Airlines) and Singapore Business News*, 9 Dec 06.

Kia Motors, Korea, made a stunning turnaround and accelerated from a deficit of 7 trillion won (US$6.2 billion) to a surplus of 180 billion won in a single year (2000). It moved from court receivership in less than 24 months. The Kia Vice President Uhm Sung-yong told Suh Hae-sung of the *Asia Times* that the answer was "tough restructuring". Apparently the number of employees was cut 30 percent to 29,000 from 40,000 and five companies were merged into one. New funds were also provided by Hyundai who took it over in 1998 when it was flat.

The Chairman of the Hyundai Group personally oversaw Kia's operations, touring production lines as often as possible and encouraging employees. This merger was a clear success and an asset to both companies, yet each retained their own individuality. Strong leadership in a time of difficulty made the difference.[26]

A turnaround expert was responsible for the breathtaking turnaround of Nissan. What made it breathtaking was he did it in just two years. A sterling example of what professional turnaround experts can do. But what he did took major surgery: He remade Nissan by eliminating what was stifling it—some business and cultural taboos. He cut Nissan's Keiretsu relationships, and revived the company's product design innovation, quality and price of product, leaving in place a new generation trained to run the new Nissan.[27]

---

[26] *Asia Times, Kia Motors completes a stunning turnaround. Suh Hae-sung 18 February 2000.*
[27] *Shift: Inside Nissan's Historic Revival, by Carlos Ghosn*, Harper Collins, 2003, and *Turnaround* by David Magee, Harper Collins (2003). *An Exploratory Study of Company Turnaround in Australia, and Singapore Following the Asia Crisis,* Springer Netherlands *(2004).*

Turnaround efforts have both worked and failed at Daimler-Chrysler over the years. Lately, largely because of Asian competition Daimler-Chrysler has moved from a profit of US$1.2 billion in 2005 to an expected loss for 2006, possibly in the billions. One of their options now is to sell or merge again, as Daimler, the true owner, needs to stop the losses, and a change of CEOs has not solved the problems. Talks of a sale to a Chinese company are now being discussed. Daimler-Chrysler believes that competitively priced small vehicles cannot be built in the U.S. The Asian companies, with flexible plants, little waste, open communication with workers, unorganized workers and a long list of loyal customers are the reasons offered.[28]

Alliances are a different proposition: a separate structure where control is not handed over. They seem to work better in the Asian business circles than in the West, but they are becoming popular in the West as well. There are many advantages: the prime one being a company is disrupted in a merger or acquisition, and much less in an alliance or joint venture.

The general rule among employees at companies is you never want to be acquired: bad things happen. If you are the acquirer, well that's better.

---

[28] *At Daimler-Chrysler the Fast Lane Is Running Downhill, New York Times, 15 December 2006*

The Asia Pacific Journal of Management, Vol. 23 (June 2006) concludes that there is a growing use of alliances and collaboration to enhance competitive advantage.

The alliance provides a way of sharing knowledge without losing control and alliances allow firms to monitor competition. They each decide what they will share and what they will not.

There are usually four parts to an alliance:
(1) Cooperation on a specific project; (2) Technology transfer with protections; (3) Facility and resource sharing, and: (4) Human resource sharing. This gives mid-sized companies the wallop of larger companies and allows them to reach their potential faster in industries that have fast moving currents of obsolescence, such as consumer marketing computer equipment and peripherals. In some cases where they may be trying to launch a breakthrough product or service and be first in the industry with it—instead by combing with another front-runner in the same industry they double their changes and find that sometimes one-half a pie is better than nothing at all.

3 Terminate the CEO; cut payroll, and negotiate with labor.

One of the mistakes of our time
is to confuse change with progress.

In the earlier part of this text we cited the destructive disease of *mimicritis,* possessed with the symptoms of blindness, anger and doing what every other patient is doing. Sacking the CEO is the prime move by inexperienced management to solve a problem. What they get out of it, it is often for very short term results and to take away pressure for a while. It is like shots of adrenalin and blood transfusions when another course of treatment must be faced. And there are times such as in the Enron Energy case where the CEO has clearly broken the company rules with fraud and secrecy amounting to criminal activity. There may be good reasons to sack the CEO, but they should be carefully examined. There are many reasons for a downturn and they cannot all be attributed to the fault of the CEO. The CEO is also in a position of knowledge and experience to help the company to better health.

Before a CEO is considered for sacking, it is time to bring in the turnaround expert. Almost all of the leading books today on the subject of corporate turnaround recommend this action. The turnaround professional can be selected using the methods that one would select a doctor if ill—the best—the experienced in the field—the recommended. This is however a relatively new profession that has historically and not too popularly been tried, by large accounting and law firms, and various kinds of corporate and financial management firms.

Managements (former patients) from other companies who have received the valued counsel of a turnaround expert or firm are choice reference centers.

In addition, graduate, university, and executive management centers such as Harvard, Wharton and the Hitachi Institute of Management Development—Japan, and the Management and Development Institute of Singapore, provide reference materials by turnaround professionals. For an understanding of the professional standards for turnaround professionals, an association for turnaround professions The International *Association of Certified Turnaround Professionals* provides an informative website and information: (http://www.actp.org).[29]

The answer on cutting payroll is it should be a demonstration of equality with the cuts across the entire organization and carefully executed via the change plan, otherwise crucial confidence and loyalty will be lost at a time when the company can ill afford it. They are an important stakeholder in making improvement work whether the company is preventing sickness or already sick.

Organized Labour Unions come in many forms depending upon the country of the company and its laws. In some countries labour has a place on the board of directors of a company. In other countries an organized union is illegal. But in the majority of the developed world they are important stakeholders in the outcome and health of the company and should be treated as such. They are not

---

[29] The International *Association of Certified Turnaround Professionals.* http://www.actp.org

the employees, yet they are—their leadership can allow them to be part of the team and fight for the team—the company—or resist and be part of a quiet civil war with management. As with all stakeholders, they must be kept in the circle of communication and action. The answer is "yes" the union should be a part of the new change. Their help will often make the difference in the success of the change. Be "above board" with them at all times is the suggestion of Jack Welch, GE Company. The leadership of labour understands that the company's health is directly related to the union and the employees' support.

In 2006 in a drastic move to keep breathing, the Ford Motor Company, coordinating with the auto workers union, offered a voluntary separation package in its process to reduce thousands of employees in its turnaround plan, This staff reduction plan means that many employees would receive the equivalent of thirteen months salary, in addition to earned pension benefits and other payouts. Going into the end of 2006, Ford has at the present forty thousand employees.

A similar solution to make a company well again has been made by state-controlled Malaysia Airlines, according to Anna Lynn Sibal, writing for *Global Watch*. The carrier has forecasted a net loss of 620 million ringgit (US$ 172 million) for 2006. They expect to cut as much as 5,000 jobs or nearly 22 percent of the airline's workforce in a plan to return to profitability in 2007. In their case buyout packages will be offered as well as was done by Ford. Ford borrowed most of the money to pay for their jobs cut, however Air Malaysia will receive some compensation from the government for theirs. This will be one of the Malaysia's largest retrenchment cases.[30]

4 Other alternative measures or resuscitation for health enhancements

Change management can improve the health of the company long before the doctor orders surgery and the crows and buzzards start forming. Here are some examples:

Note: The footnotes below from numbers 31 through 43 are for cases in previous pages and chapters in this book. See below for case names:

-Bringing in an independent board of directors to review major decisions.[31]

-Selling the company real estate then leasing it back or parts of it.[32]

-Selling non-core product divisions that are not profitable.[33]

-Considering licensing certain products, designs or services to other companies.[34]

-Borrowing the necessary turnaround money while conditions are still stable.[35]

-Establishing communications systems that work: such as setting up a blog[36] between the CEO, management, and employees.

- Organizing offshore, lower cost design and product development.[37]

-Setting the first essential change event to occur within sixty days in the plan.

---

[30] *"Malaysia Air to Lay off 22% Off Work Force,"* Anna Lynn Sibal, *Global Watch.* http://gbwatch.com
[31] Four Seasons, supra
[32] Enron Energy
[33] GE Int'l
[34] Ford
[35] British Petroleum
[36] Daimler-Chrysler
[37] Korean Bank

-Prioritizing cash flow potentials

-Inviting private equity companies: cautious territory.[38]

-Finding help by merging.[39]

-Creating buyouts, sell-outs, and alliances.[40]

-Negotiating with creditors and litigants.[41]

-Crisis management options, such as bankruptcy as last resort planning.[42]

-Technology update and audit.[43]

-Implement turnaround plan phase II with turnaround expert. See the following cases.

Change should not be confused with Progress

The McKinsey Quarterly in a recent issue interviewed a CEO about the CEO's experience rehabilitating a company. The CEO noted that the company that was turned around had a profitable licensing agreement that disguised the cash flow and caused cost problems. There were 42,000 people employed by the European company when he arrived and 27,000 when health was restored—yet, the company's output was roughly the same. The streamlining was conventional: closing down plants, reducing overheads, and other restructuring efforts.

---

[38] Kia Motors
[39] ENI
[40] Nissan, Qantas Airlines
[41] Enron Energy
[42] Northwest Airlines
[43] Nissan

In another case the same CEO, rescued the direction of a company by following his philosophy that had paid off for him in managing change many times, and that was his premise that the change team must keep things simple. For example, when he took over as CEO of his current company the company had become a 'kind of conglomerate'. "It was active in many sectors. What we did was to refocus around the core businesses of gas and electricity and divest the remainder to get rid of the distractions. We cleaned the table, as I like to put it.

If you have too many problems to think about, you cannot cope with all of them. I like to reduce the complexity in a business. It is a restructuring strategy. If it takes more than one minute to explain a strategy, something is wrong."
The CEO also commented on the idea that departments of a company should be profit centers. "A mistake can be made, which is to turn cost centers like IT, engineering, and real estate into stand-alone profit centers. By their very nature some are non-competitive."

Also, in the interview with Giancario Ghislanzoni, a director with McKinsey in the Milan, Italy office, the CEO emphasized the important role that good communication in the turnaround company requires. "I am convinced that communication is a very powerful tool for running a large organization. It works fine if people know exactly where they are going, but in order to know this they need to grasp some easy concepts (the need to keep things simple) and repeat, repeat, repeat."[44] The CEO's current company is not a turnaround company (Eni), the number one gas company in Europe. But I'm sure that Mr. Scaroni would agree improvement is a daily must for sustaining the health of a company whether it is sick or healthy. And that is one of the themes of this writing. On the other hand, I'm sure he would be the first to agree that the old adage of "Don't fix it if it doesn't need fixin,'" applies as well.

The world sees Toyota Motor Corp., as an unstoppable profit company that may replace General Motors as the world's largest auto maker. But the CEO of Toyota is not resting on these trophies and laurels. He is known for his fierce insistence on efficiency, and just because his company is now in front, he does not let up with what has been his successful DNA drive for the company. CEO Katsuaki Watanabe, has warned that Toyota may be losing its competitive edge around the world. He wonders if the company's factories are efficient enough. He has even questioned a core tenet of Toyota's culture—*kaisen, The Wall Street Journal—Asia Edition,* reported in December, 2006.[45]

---

[44] An interview with Paola Scaroni, CEO of Europe's number one gas company, Eni, by Giancarlo Ghislanzoni, a director, McKinsey & Company, Milan, Italy in the *McKinsey Quarterly, December 2006.*
[45] *"As Rivals Catch Up, Toyota CEO Spurs Big Efficiency Drive,"* Norimiko Shirouzu, Asia-Edition of the Wall Street Journal, December, 2006.

Taking what CEOs Mr. Wantanabe (Toyota) and Mr. Scaroni (Eni) believe and practice, the steps of turnaround are not patented tools of the very sick, but are used across the board in healthy as well as sick companies. This should be the considered philosophy folded into the next topic of implementing a change or turnaround program.

Temasek Holdings Pte., is a successful Singapore financial and investment management company in Singapore which has US$83bil of assets, and their management move is worthwhile noting in terms of how a company can become well or if well, continue to sustain its health. Toward the end of 2006 they rotated and reassigned responsibilities in the company as part of a staff development program. And apparently they rotated key managers before 2002 and 2005.[46]

---

[46] *Star Publications (Malaysia) Bhd,* December, 2006.

5 When Company Faces Problems: Bankruptcy as a last Result

We have discussed the bankruptcy topic in earlier turnaround examples. It is considered as the last resort, but an important one. While certain answers turn up by visiting the morgue, the better place to learn what is ailing the patient is in the hospital while the patient is still alive. With companies it is the same. And the bankruptcy option can be a floating piece of rescue on an ocean of mean waves, or an exit into dark waters.

Kia Motors of Korea is an excellent example of the bankruptcy working in partnership with the turnaround process, and that is the recommended course of treatment to take. In Asian nations, because of tradition and culture, bankruptcy is indeed the last result—and this is most commendable. For it allows time for the company to find itself, and for the turnaround doctors to treat the patient to wellness. However, how the bankruptcy process will proceed in China is at this time only a guess. Its success will require that the citizens have confidence that the courts will provide a just system free of governmental interference; until that happens it will be impossible to achieve the goals of a proper bankruptcy process.

In the West, however, it is not, unfortunately, the same. Too often the patient is subjected to major surgery when alternative medicine would have been the healer. What happens in bankruptcy? The big point is *Control*—the company loses it to the court and to the creditors. The end result may be putting the company and all it stands for—up for auction. The scavengers dive in: the private equity funds, adventure capitalists, competitors, often not to run the company but to tear it apart and sell its bones at the highest price. Bankruptcy should not be an early option in the turnaround process.

CHAPTER SIX— Accounting and Financial Consideration

Chapter topics

1. **What Is Not Seen On The Balance Sheet?**

2. **The Case of Enron**

3. **Does The Accounting Balance Reflect Reality?**

1. What Is Not Seen On The Balance Sheet?

One of the largest companies in recent times, one that we have mentioned earlier, collapsed on the supposed road to grand success. The case taught us that it is what's NOT on the balance sheet and financial statements that can be the most important in the health of a company. The global energy trading giant Enron collapsed into bankruptcy in 2001.

Enron was ranked by *Fortune* Magazine as one of the "most admired" in the world. The company shareholders lost billions of dollars of their hard-earned savings in the collapse. The turnaround team was called in late, after most of the damage was done: it was like sharing the patient's hospital room with the spiritual giver of the last rites to the patient while the autopsy team was waiting outside the door, according to a member of the turnaround team in the court records.

In examining the trial record of the case, a criminal trial against the CEO and other management officials of Enron, the court was troubled by the fact that the government officials overlooked for years Enron's misconduct: they were apparently not victims of too little information, but probably too much—of the wrong kind. Analysts simply failed to make sense of the data supplied. This is a shocking conclusion when one considers how little shareholders know what is really happening to their investments.

Enron was using an accounting method called mark-to-market accounting. Suppose your company enters into an agreement with ABC Electric to deliver them five-hundred-thousand-dollars (US$) of electricity (five-million-kilowatt hours) in the year 2009. How much is that contract worth in the accounting year in which it was signed (2007)? Payment would not be until 2009. Whether or not there would be a profit or loss would not be known until 2009. If electricity production costs increase as 2009 has approached the deal could be a loser. If they went the other way, a considerable profit would be the yield.

With mark-to-market accounting, you estimate how much revenue the deal is going to bring in and put that number in your books at the moment you sign the contract. If down the line, the estimate is off, you adjust the balance sheet to correct the figures. Enron showed billions of dollars on their balance sheet in this form of a transaction. The balance sheets were certified by one of the largest accounting firms in the world (Arthur Andersen & Co.).

The next major question, the one it finally took the turnaround experts to hone in on was: How much of the huge sums Enron was making was "real".

In times of illness and distress companies are tempted to use this cover-up method of accounting, which can hide the real truths of a company's performance. And in Enron's case massive egotism and criminal minds dealt the morality cards. The Hippocratic Oath for business was forgotten.

2. The Case of Enron

The other problem with Enron's accounting was a heavy reliance on S.P.Es (Separate Partnership Entities) . An S.P.E is a separate partnership with another company. The other partners may be other investors. An example would be as follows: A company's sales are down; their cash flow is running very low; they are heavily in debt. If they could find a loan it would be at the highest rate of interest. But the company holds a number of mineral leases that are handed over to the partnership (S.P.E). The bank then loans millions of dollars to the partnership and the partnership gives the money back to the company. At the time (2001) in the USA this transaction did NOT have to be reported on the balance sheet. The company can therefore raise capital without increasing its indebtedness. In some cases, such as in Enron's case Enron managed the partnerships with their own management. It was a closed circuit deal among related parties.

These S.P.Es have become commonplace in the corporate world along with other techniques that makes diagnosis, treatment, and recovery difficult.

3. Does The Accounting Balance Reflect Reality?

One journalist following the Enron investigation concluded that if you believe you are starting to enter a game of hide and seek as you review a company's financial statements and balance sheets—you probably are.

As it turned out, the examination of the S.P.E. entities came to a summary of twenty thousand single spaced pages. *There were 3000 such partnerships*! What the lessons of Enron prove is that corporate disclosures (and it made them as required) can be only icing on the cake.

From a public filed accounting and investor standpoint Enron was in the black millions of dollars. Why was it that they never paid or owed any income taxes?

And since this went on for five years or more why didn't someone ask the question? No one did. It was the turnaround experts that saw it. A simple but a profound question. According to the Internal Revenue Service accounting (the Federal US taxing authority) they owed nothing and paid nothing because they made nothing!

CHAPTER SEVEN—International Trade Options for Turnaround Companies.

Chapter Topics

1. Currency

2. Trade Barriers

3. Labour

4. Tax structures

5. Regional Trade Alliances

6. Governmental Action/political stability

7. Rogue Disorder

8. Natural Disasters/Environmental concerns

9. Intellectual property

10. The internet/communications/security

11. Human Rights and Environmental considerations

If a company is not involved in international trade in some ways and it is operating in an industry that is touched by international trade—in the current world of globalization—doing business internationally should be a mandatory consideration for any company sick or healthy.

1. Currency

The currency chosen for international transactions is a negotiable item between the seller and the buyer. The goal is to establish the contracts in the most stable currency available to the parties to prevent fluctuations one way or the other.

Should the payment be due in all or part at the signing of the agreement, the date the equipment is completed or acquired by the seller, or the date it is delivered, or the date it performs successfully on a performance test. At what event does the payment occur; this will be an important one for currency values as they may shift up or down with either the seller or the buyer's currency?

This needs to be well outlined in the Agreement between the buyer and seller. It makes an international transaction, along with other factors more complex than a domestic-only one. For example, a complicated product like a supercomputer will take six months to a year to build in some cases and with shipping, installation and performance standards, the money may not be due in some cases for a year after the order.

Each party will want the currency that is most available to them and that they can depend upon for stable values. Only the large companies can usually play the game of betting on currency fluctuations, because it is not the work of amateurs. What is the general rule for companies to control fluctuation is to clearly set forth the values of the currency involved in the transaction on a certain date, such as the date of delivery—then there is no guessing and pricing can be established along with profit analysis by both parties.

2. Trade Barriers

The World Trade Organization's (WTO) has a major goal of eliminating trade barriers between companies to allow for a free flow of goods and monies in and out of countries. They have been only minimally successful to date. Although some countries have lowered customs, tariffs and quotas, they have often been replaced by other disguised barriers such as taxes, fees, subsidies, and inspections.

It is the government of the country that must balance the interests of its commerce system and its people, the workers. To throw thousands of its hard working citizens out of work without supporting them with other employment or benefits until they can find new work is unethical. And certain trade barriers need to be gradually eased. We have already mentioned the high cost of exporting rice to Indonesia and Japan where the duties favor the native growers and keep imports out. And we have pointed out the rationale for this. It is a commodity that is crucial to their peoples' survival. If a famine would occur the UN estimates that there are stored supplies available to last less than a year in the best of conditions.[47]

---

[47] UN Statistics (2004)

Trade barriers conceal themselves in many ways: one way is through extra red tape coming through a border, and another way is through inspections. With the scares of rogue disorder, diseases, dangerous foods, and other unsafe products, many of the inspections required today that are costly to both the buyer and the seller are necessary, but there is the question of discrimination now and then that favors domestic products over foreign products.

3. Labor

Jack Welch (GE) advises to be always honest and straight with labor; stand one's ground or nobody will have a job if the company doesn't make money. We've covered some labor examples in an earlier part of this book dealing with the importance of labor's cooperation in either a turnaround situation or in improving a healthy company. Good employees are often the heart of a company.

And consumers, the customers, recognize the employees' value because they are often much closer to the employees than the CEO and the Board. Many a business has gone from health to sickness because of their treatment of the employees. This is one factor that the customers pick up very quickly and easily. And in case after case they penalize a company that treats its employees poorly. And many businesses have gone from sickness to health because they have considered their employees as part of the team.

Both Japan and Germany in restructuring their labor laws included labor in the governance of a company. It would seem to be a wise move based upon their cultures and success. A strike by labor is very devastating. Some countries restrict the usage of strikes if the public interest is involved. There is a rating system that is used by management on whether to invest in a business in a new country that rates the number of strikes or labour unrest incidents in the country. If the rating is high the country is a known labour risk country.

4. Tax structures

Taxes are one aspect of commerce that can change greatly. It is often under the political umbrella of influence that is unpredictable. But in the midst of a recovery or improvement, or if as part of that process a company participates in international trade, taxes may govern their decisions on how they design and operate.

The good news is that the international tax structure is not prohibitively complex. Agreements between developed countries provide a reasonable platform of dividing taxes on transactions and products crossing borders. The exporting company must decide whether or not they will be "doing business" in the offshore country or participate in infrequent transactions. While it is not healthy business practice to do business dictated to by the tax gods, these decisions are financially important and the experts need to be summoned to answer these legal and tax questions.

Taxes can also be the healing friend of the company. A number of governmental units both national and local in many countries offer tax benefits to companies if they do business there, remain there, or move there. Unpaid taxes often complicate a turnaround process greatly: they must be dealt with early and with the help of expertise when a sick company owes various taxes. The worst reaction is to ignore them. And in most countries they are not dischargeable via bankruptcy. It is true that death and taxes are a reality that cannot be escaped, luckily, however, taxes can be managed—and death too—with the right doctors—at least for some good years.

5. Regional Trade Alliances

One of the more successful trade alliances in the world is the Association of South East Asian Nations (ASEAN) trade alliance of Southeast Asian countries.

Along with the ASEAN trade alliance, the North American Free Trade Area (NAFTA) has also achieved a free flow of commerce between its members. For those who want to be one world organization, such as the World Trade Organization, they are not in favor of a number of regional trade alliances making trade rules as they were formed. The WTO was formed to try and solve problems and promote world trade, and regional organizations are apparent competitors.

A regional trade association plan seems competitive. But it has not worked out to be competition. It is human nature that neighbors find their mutual problems and solutions are better attended to by neighbors—so too, in nations. These alliances can provide new markets for struggling companies and companies on the path to improvement, as these alliances allow for shipment of products and services between the members at less cost in the form of quotas, duties and taxes. They also provide a global forum for the representation of concerns and solutions for their member nations, and as a bloc.

6. Governmental action/Political instability.

What government does is important to a company's health. A CEO and management must keep watch over how government or governments may change their business. This watch is extremely important while a company is trying to get or continue to be well. In centrally controlled economies the government is really the third party to every contract. The good news is that governmental actions are often very helpful for a struggling company.

In examining a number of turnarounds it becomes clear that markets are being missed. This may or may not be the reason for the company's need to change. However, the largest buyers in most countries are governmental buyers. There are few countries, such as the U.S. that have retained the medical industry and national medical care as a private business. This is true, also with airlines in the U.S. These two major areas have remained privatized—never owned publicly. The marketing of product to these two industries is quite different and allows for much opportunity to a company with products or services in those two huge industries. What governments do or don't do becomes central in many marketing plans and turnaround strategies.

India for example has from time to time stopped the sales of state-owned companies. This is not unusual for a country on the tip of moving into more privatization, but this could wreck certain plans for company expansion, because also there is the concern by banks and investors that the larger program of economic change that is planned in India will be bogged down in politics.[48]

Governmental actions may enhance or upset company plans, and in turnaround plans. When the heavy VCR tax went off, most VCRs in countries opened up the way for consumers to purchase them at reasonable prices in country after country. The cinemas of the world lost the fight. Enter—the video producers, film, and video rental businesses across the globe, and millions of buying consumers! For those companies that scoped this in their strategy for their future, they became hugely successful.

---

[48] *India Stops Privation,* Saritha Rai, 11 July 2006 New York Times

The question is often when is a government going to act? In 2006 the US Congress approved normalizations of trade with Vietnam, clearing the way for Vietnam to become a member of the World Trade Organization, giving an enormous economic boost to the country by increased opportunities of exports. But the issue was pending for ten years! For companies depending upon this decision to increase or save their businesses, this was a long wait.

A factor to be considered in turnaround options: governmental action at all levels can boost or bust the turnaround, or in the Vietnam case can force them to find other markets for their exports.

Turnaround examples are not always obvious and may come in different forms. An excellent example is Japan during the decade of the nineties. And Japan's turnaround was clearly Japanese. Governments in turnarounds are helpful to study for all in the turnaround realm. Companies are micros of governments. Japan's economy in 2006 is the world's second largest ($4.7 trillion) after the United States and one of the top three or four militaries.

In the 1980s and before Japan seemed to be immune to any economic sicknesses. In the 1990s the annual growth of 8% in the 80s fell just as fast as its terrific health had gained. Like a tsunami the state guided economy could not be stopped during a decade of stagnation since the late 1980s, suffering stock market and real estate crashes.

But since 2002 Japan has been on a rebounding turnaround. It has been concluded Japan's declining decade was not a sickness but a restructuring period. Japan companies halt the downfall and began new programs: They sold subsidiaries that were expense holes, moved production abroad, and expanded merit based compensation.

The Japanese government played a role in the turnaround as well by modifying the pension system, revised corporate law, and removed a stack of bad loans. Then it reorganized itself as well.

They followed the German style of restructuring labour rather than that of the UK or the US which includes representatives of labour in the governance of the company. The plus side of this is strikes and labour disputes have been kept to a minimum and communication of the health of the company is more a part of a team effort throughout the entire company. Japanese companies have benefited from low turnover of employees. This is often a critical factor in a company's health. However, in the U.S. labor has few rights in the governance of the company and therefore labour is not integrated into the governance of the company. American corporations have nearly the right of complete freedom in hiring and firing employees. The result often is the only alternative labour has for change of policy on wages and benefits is a strike. However, what works for one culture may not for another. Although the labour laws of the U.S. have shifted over time with elections, the culture and voters have upheld the right of the companies to control their business and to generally keep the government out of business.

Japanese companies have also turned away from mergers and acquisitions to solve turnaround and growth problems. In the U.S. mergers and acquisitions make big headlines almost on a daily basis for the industrial news media such as the Wall Street Journal and other business publications. Company statements in Japan indicate that they see mergers and acquisition as disruptive and gimmicky. And in supplier shopping for the lowest cost, the vice chairman of NEC has recently stated: "If you just procure what is the cheapest then what do you do about the cost of developing the next technology. The concept of social harmony is a theme of the Japan turnaround and is valued because it provides a valued sense of harmony and develops a more long term value.

In a restructuring process, some things may change and some things may not. In the Japanese process the Japan model discriminates against the largest section of their temporary work force—women. Industrial collusion is fostered, which would be an anathema in the U.S. and other countries, and the Japanese model cheats their consumers out of cheaper imports. However, there are variations to the post 1990s model internally in Japan, for example, the telecom industry

While globalization seems like an escaping animal in a circus that will never be tamed, there is nevertheless a strong divergence based upon cultures and nationalities; no one country model dominates. Common sense dictates this to be the wisest course. Certainly there will be changes in the way business and government work themselves out in such countries as Communist ruled China.

In China, its economic and political health will be determined by governmental action, as it is a centrally planned economy by government. Change will only come when similar headlines like the following from the New York Times change:

Articles in this series examine the struggle in China over the creation of a modern legal system.

In Worker's Death, View of China's Harsh Justice
By JIM YARDLEY
There is widespread suspicion, even within the government, that too many innocent people are sentenced to death.
December 31, 2005

When Chinese Sue the State, Cases Are Often Smothered
By JOSEPH KAHN
Courts often refuse to issue any verdict at all - or even acknowledge that some legal complaints exist.
December 28, 2005

Seeking a Public Voice on China's 'Angry River'
By JIM YARDLEY
A proposal for a dam project is now unexpectedly presenting the Chinese government with a quandary of its own making: will it abide by its own laws?
December 26, 2005

Legal Gadfly Bites Hard, and Beijing Slaps Him
By JOSEPH KAHN
GAO Shushing has become the most prominent in a string of outspoken

lawyers facing persecution.
December 13, 2005

A Judge Tests China's Courts, Making History
By JIM YARDLEY
A ruling on a mundane case about seed prices opened a debate on judicial autonomy in China's political system.
November 28, 2005

Desperate Search for Justice: One Man vs. China
By JIM YARDLEY
A father's quest to free his son poses a question about China: Is it possible for a criminal defendant to get a fair trial?
November 12, 2005

Dispute Leaves U.S. Executive in Chinese Legal Nether world
By JOSEPH KAHN
In China, where the legal system rarely backs investors or ordinary citizens against the state, an entrepreneur has become a pawn in a commercial dispute.
November 1, 2005

Deep Flaws, and Little Justice, in China's Court System
By JOSEPH KAHN
Forced confessions remain endemic in a judicial system that faces pressure to maintain "social stability" at all costs.
September 21, 2005

In the fall of 2006 the U.S. voters elected a new government that is heavily tied to labour unions, and that will take office in January of 2007. Business is worried that this new government may be susceptible to protectionism to protect jobs from import competition. Since the economies of the developed nations are now globalized the cause and effect of protectionism will directly control national economies in matters of international business as well as national business.

In December of 2006, Indonesia announced that they would not cut the price of rice by allowing it to be imported. This is sometimes referred to as trade barrier. But like the high import tax on VCRs in the eighties, trade barriers come and go. A futuristic turnaround expert often has such opportunities in sight.

Be the first in when the barriers go down is the general rule. It would be a long wait, however, probably for Indonesia, as well as other Asian countries before imported rice is allowed, much to the World Trade Commission's chagrin. But the protection is understandable when one considers that tradition and caution for the future feeding of the population is at stake. Yet, on the other hand it may be an opportunity for the Native American tribes who have not been successful in exporting wild rice (tan colored) harvested naturally from the pristine lakes of Canada and the northern part of the U.S.—because it is not really a rice—it's technically a grass.

The Asian financial crisis prompted the Monetary Authority of Singapore (MAS) to establish an agency to help banks prevent credit card loan defaults amid a rise in personal and small business bankruptcies. It was planned to start in September 2002. Such efforts by government demonstrate one of the innovative ways that government can support the financial integrity of a country's financial and consumer citizens.[49]

---

[49] *Asian Economic News,* 4 Feb 2002

A similar boost to help people and therefore the country and the businesses of that country was announced in December of 2006 by the Asia Development Bank to loan US$1bn to India for the poor, particularly in the country's agricultural sector.[50]

Although there is some help by government to the people (the consumers) by the governments of the world, and some of this help extends to small and large businesses as well—coming in different forms from loans, to grants, to subsidies, and tax breaks, but the turnaround recovery is largely the work of the company and its change experts with little help from government.

In China there are many state owned companies that perhaps need to be turned around, changed and brought through the funnel of what this writing has prescribed for sick companies. It will not be easy, and since these companies are so tied into and intertwined with other state companies the maze will have to be undone skillfully, so unemployment and confusion will not strike the country. It is hoped the government will retain turnaround counsel with experience to work together with them in the task.

---

[50] *Financial Times, Asia-Pacific*, 10 December 2006.

Political stability is a fundamental building block to entering the global marketplace. From a dictatorship a country can spin into anarchy and gangster capitalism. The predictability rate of what is happening and what is going to happen is crucial. It is needed by big and small and turnaround companies alike to prevent further risks.

Before the terrible tsunami waves hit Aceh, Indonesia in December of 2004 there was some progress towards peace between the Rebels and the Indonesian Army. This has been remarkable since this tragedy, peace between the two factions has become a reality and hopes are the 29 year conflict will end. The winners will be the people, their children and the nation. Soon commerce will enrich the area as conflict destroys the fabric of the people and builds a fence to the outer world of trade and communications.[51]

7. Rogue disorder

The history of humanity has always been able to provide the current generation with the threat of an Apocalypse: a poison on human life. This is a ticket to the bankruptcy court for lawful and ethical business. The headlines on the world's TV screens and the print of the media carry this awful message daily of the turmoil around the globe by rogues. These villains change costumes and masks from one time in history to another, but they are all the same: they are usually controlled, as if automatons by mad and criminal people and forces.

---

[51] *In Tsunami's Wake, Old Foes In War Now Wage Politics,* Seth Mydans, *New York Times 12/06*

These rogues currently poison commerce. In certain parts of the world they are nearly so, or are in control, and the solution will be resolved by political or military means, not business. Although being optimistic, there are many instances in recent history where old enemies have become friends because they have finally communicated with each other via their business interests and transactions (China, Vietnam, Japan, Russia, and the U.S.).

A poem was recently published about Rogue Disorders by an Irish poet:

Peace

When the evil ones admit
Their evil
Then it will be all over
Fear will disappear.
Earth will be paradise again.

When will all this happen Grandpa?
I think it's coming;
You just wait and see.

No use bothering yourself
About these idiots running around today
Pointing fingers and quacking into the wind.
OK?

But we are still trying to follow the imminently wise counsel of Confucius to achieve harmony and peace in the world. And the temperature rises and falls each day on this measurement.

8. Natural disasters/Environmental Concerns

Change needs to be the keyword in the care plan for a sick company. Jack Welch the former CEO of GE (General Electric) has emphasized in his books and speeches that creativity and change are the main steps to recovery. But in planning, the whole process of recovery can be clicked on PAUSE by a natural disaster, or as the maritime insurance policies say "Acts of God." Tsunamis, hurricanes, and earthquakes are horrible, life-taking, and disastrous to business.

Even with the latest supercomputers that are expert machines on analyzing seismic and meteorological events, the prediction results are still very risky. And even if they are accurate in warning of a catastrophe, humans by nature are going to generally ignore it (Hurricane Katrina, USA—July 2005).

And in the tsunami that killed, it is estimated 170,000 people, in December 2004 in Indonesia left a half a million people homeless. The horror of this tragedy is difficult to describe. Two years later only one-half of the replacement homes that were promised and planned have been constructed. The same discouraging percentage of completion is true also in the New Orleans (Katrina) area of the U.S. Turnarounds are not limited to business; governmental units also need to turnaround to protect their people. Much change management is required to prevent these catastrophes from such a heavy loss of life.

There is a movement that is considerably well-intentioned that is operating in the world, in developed countries and undeveloped countries, and asserting that global warming will change the way we live, where we live, and if we live.

The Global Network of Agricultural Research Centres (CGIAR) is an organization that links 15 research institutes around the world. According to the BBC correspondent Richard Black they have stated that rice yields in South Asia are declining yearly. The largest impact on crops of climate change in Agriculture is probably changes in rainfall—some regions are receiving less and some regions too much. There is also an impact on plants and their photosynthesis, which becomes slower as the temperature rises. A new breed of rice is needed to speed up rice photosynthesis in order for countries to produce enough to feed their peoples if this group is correct. They also forecast that the vast South Asia wheat yield that produces about 15 % of the world's wheat will shrink to about one-half the current production in the next 50 years.[52]

If the global warming forecasts are true, commerce and businesses can be ruined unless they change while interruption of contracts, orders, and life itself—stops. These risks can happen anywhere on the planet and do. Some may be anticipated and planned, but most cannot. And they can arrive on the day for turnaround companies, and for others, when there is no doctor to help. Reliance on strictly current data and information along with expert counsel often is able to ease the risk for some of these catastrophes. And when they are

---

[52] *New Crops Needed To Avoid Famines,* Richard Black, *BBC website,* 3 December 2006.

rescued--in time-- but certainly the rescue from a tragedy does not pass quickly in the minds and memories of the people, there is much rebuilding to do and for the survivors including the companies in need of change and turnaround-- considerable work is available.

But the global warming issues are still to being examined by the doctors as disagreements exist on the causes and remedies at this time. However, what is not debated is the fact that increased carbon dioxide, whatever the reason, warms the earth and causes weather changes. The natural diet of plants is carbon dioxide; however, the plant population has not kept up with the human population. If the emissions of carbon dioxide are to be controlled, the patients spreading the most emissions on the planet, which some consider to be a serious infection, will have to take the lead for change—and those patients are called China, India, and the U.S.

Environmental laws and practice in a country may well decide how and where they can export their products. The EC (European Community) via their parliament are considering trade barriers against imports from countries with high carbon dioxide levels and with only inactive environmental protection levels.

9. Intellectual property laws

In the world of commerce the inventions, designs, writings, and product developments of a company are often its richest assets. The best way of protecting them is to be the first on the market with the new concept or product. Preceding this goal, of course, is the registration of the patent, trademark or copyright, first in the country of the company and then in a country or countries where the company intends to do business.

In some Asian companies, such as Japan, the first to file for intellectual property protection has the prior claim, even though the product had been invented in another country and registered in that country first. This procedure is the opposite from the U.S. intellectual property law process in that the first to file may not have a prior claim—it is not run like a race—the first to file wins.

When a company is sick, its intellectual property can be a hidden asset: it is used in collateral for loans, it is franchised, and it is leased, or is correctly appraised to show a proper asset or financial statement. This special property is often an attractive reason why successful alliances, joint ventures, and mergers work well.

Countries that do not adopt to modern ways or enforce their intellectual property laws run the risk of losing businesses and investment capital that would otherwise come if their key assets, their intellectual property is safe. In improving a company this is one aspect that cannot be overlooked. When sick it is the worst time for a patient to have a thief sneak into the room and take valuables from the sick. So too, with a company—while struggling or trying to improve it cannot take the hit of losing its key properties.

China has made considerable progress in modernizing its intellectual property laws, and made progress in enforcing them. This is important because membership in the Word Trade Organization (WHO) depends upon this protection. Ironically, there are more intellectual property piracy cases in the US courts than in any other country.

10. Internet/communications security

In an interview with Dr. Tian Yuan, Chairman of the China Chengtong Holding Company, *Business-in-Asia* quizzed him about how he saw the prospects for companies doing business in China via the internet? His reply was stated as follows:

> *We think the real successful companies in the Internet business in China will be those that can serve or combine their internet operations with other parts of their traditional businesses or industries ("old economy"). Businesses that solely have an internet focus without a production or other old economy element will*

find it very hard to succeed[53].

In a turnaround, where the improvement of the company is the goal, as well as in healthy companies trying to improve, the marketing and advertising potential of the internet is an attractive option. But the ones on the front lines of the world's businesses would agree with Dr. Tian Yuan, that the internet has NOT changed the way business is done.

Technology will never change the fact that a company has to know and trust who they are doing business with, confirm the quality of the products or services, and negotiate the best transaction. However, it is true that the internet has changed one thing clearly, and that is the *relationship* between the company and the customer. There is now the possibility of a direct line between the two and just not through dealers, agents, retail outlets, and distributors. A good example is Dell computers. The questions of value—what value will the internet give to my company?—and also to my clients? What benefit is it to my company? These questions need to be clearly answered before taking the internet cure for a company's operations.

In planning the use of the internet as a global tool a company must realize that there are certain laws and limitations when one crosses a border—and this is true where one walks across a country border or crosses it electronically. Just like in days of telefax, there are always the big ears to guard against—and security is a needed investment whether the system is an internal network

---

[53] *Interview with Dr. Tian Yuan, Chairman of China Chengtong Holding Co.* Business-in-Asia.com, 12/06.

system throughout the world or stands alone. In certain countries today certain words, products, services will draw governmental attention and in some blocked. None of this is good for business. All of this costs money to prevent.

The last thing a company needs when it is looking to expand its sales is to start out in a country with internet violations. There are border crossing these times of both kinds: software that limits the internet and software that tries to skip the blocks. International efforts to govern this aspect of communication have so far not succeeded.[54]

For a company to expect a turnaround from using the internet to sell its products it must first develop messages that are not subject to "Spam" filters and "Click Fraud Detectors". Most businesses and millions of potential customers now restrict messages severely to predetermined lists through Spam filters. In addition, if a message exceeds two clicks--three clicks (strikes) and you are out. The future could well be that internet messages will only be received by the party welcoming them ahead of time.

If business in a country is going to prosper the government must keeps its hands (and ears) off the Internet. No wise investor or company can take the risk of exposing their crucial intellectual property and trade operation secrets to a government. A government that is so defensive that it controls the internet is also a corrupt and unstable government that will either become more democratic

---

[54] MBA Notes, Zelium International, 2005.

or its monopoly will be broken by its citizens in a revolution of some kind, hopefully political election and peaceful.

A report from the Hitachi/Wharton School of Management indicates that internet is crucial to healthy as well as sick businesses. The day will soon be here that sales to customers and suppliers will require the internet for orders and sales completions. Internet usages have increased the productivity of companies by a considerable extent. And this is what a turnaround company exactly needs.

Being in E-commerce is one of the first steps to rehabilitation for some companies. Both Government and Industry are relying more and more on internet based orders. The whole use of design and product improvement with offshore companies is dependent upon the internet for communications. And this is one of the options we have presented for turnaround innovation.

Similarly problems of high cost: the high cost product production and high cost labour can also be improved via outsourcing and management of it via the internet. While internet, like all technologies has certain limitations and threats, no turnaround would be complete without a significant technological audit on how the company could improve by full utilization of the internet.[55]

---

[55] Hitachi/Wharton, *Back to the Basics in the New Internet Economy.* An interview with the CEO of CISCO, Mr. John Chambers, August 2006. *Knowledge-Wharton.*

The internet can be a company's friend or foe. In the recent example of Proctor & Gamble in China it has been a big problem. Proctor & Gamble manufactures a product called SK II and the market in China for the product was strong and growing stronger as the Chinese family is able to purchase what was a formerly considered high luxury product just a few years ago. Proctor & Gamble estimates that 7% of their world sales came from China for the SK II product.

What is the product problem? Pressure from the government and the Chinese consumers that came after tests had shown that some samples of the product had caused some skin problems. How did the world get around? Well, the service of internet and thousands of potential consumers in Proctor & Gamble. Blogs carried the message that caused the company to withdraw the product from the market as trust in the product was quickly lost. Management did not apologize and the destruction landed. The company, that had produced products that had been trusted by the Chinese consumers for many years, now faces a major need for turnaround.

The freedom of the internet may bring its downfall. Google, the giant internet search company has been on an aggressive campaign since its founding less than a decade ago to keep the internet free of political and governmental or rogue influence. It is upsetting to internet users to see Google appease a government in order to enter that country's market and cooperate with that country's government in suppressing the freedom of the internet, which cause security concerns for people and companies. Such unethical actions will destroy the internet and any business dependent upon it.

11. Human Rights and the Environment

You may ask what these topics are doing in a Corporate Turnaround book with a Global Prospective. Membership in the World Trade Organization grants many privileges and rights to its country members and their citizens in the world trade marketplace as well as in the human communities of the world. A country that ignores the rights of human beings and the future of its children due to environmental carelessness will be rebuffed by the world and such organizations as the World Trade Organizations. Slave labour, child labour, gender discrimination, laws that are cruel and inhuman, will be resisted by the hammer of economics. China, for example, was admitted to the World Trade Organization on the basis that it would defend the human rights of its citizens. Countries that continue to practice an inhuman or bigoted culture will simply face trade barriers and restrictions on any exports they try to make. Their companies will pay the price as well as their citizens.

Jack Welch (GE) concludes that most innovations come from the suggestions and needs of the company's customers. It does not take a multi-million dollar research budget to develop them. And Thomas Edison, the inventor of the light bulb and a thousand other patents, advised that most innovations are found accidentally by working on something else. The key phrase is to have the flexibility to be working on something new. And here is the new industry that can use products from the old industry for many uses once they have been "greened" comes in handy for a company in a turnaround and in need of a new shot of adrenalin in the form of a new product or service.

As many change management texts have advised: In a recovery mode there is no better time to come up with something new—a new product or service. An example is in the present medical, aerospace and also as stated, the energy and environmental fields. Consider that thousands of new products will be needed in these fields. Consider that this may be the time for your company to throw down the crutches of selling only commodity products and enter these fields. Products and companies come and go those that stay welcome expertise and change.

An example is Beijing, China today: According to *Breitbart News,* every monitoring station in Beijing's urban districts recorded levels of particulates seven times higher than the safety standard, according to the Beijing environmental protection bureau. People who are feeble, old or the young are advised to stay in their houses. China is recognizing they must make a turnaround about pollution. Where are the companies that can help China to solve this problem? They will come, and probably some will be your competitors. Every problem has a challenge. But the alert and talented companies have historically been known to solve it.

There is a higher purpose adrenalising environmental groups today, and that is to create an environment that is independent of petroleum, particularly foreign petroleum. And it will also bring with it many new opportunities for turnaround businesses to provide the market new products as has already started to occur in recent years and that we have examined in this book as an option to a company in need of new products for growth reasons and to stave off competition or escape from the possibly the well worn marketplace they are locked into. But even with huge investments in alternative fuels, complete independence from oil won't happen for many decades.

There seems to be a kind of utopian daydream running through both the halls of power in Washington and Brussels and the informal meeting rooms of environmentalists. The former covet independence from oil, or at least foreign oil, for political reasons: the latter, for humanitarian, medical, and business reasons. This market of new products has already started to occur in recent years. It is a positive bit of news and an option to a company in turnaround, and to all companies. But more than that, it is good news for our lungs, our children, and our health.

CHAPTER EIGHT—Part I. Summary

Harmony would lose its attractiveness
if it did not have a background of discord.
-Tehyi Hsieh, *Chinese Epigrams*

Many global enterprises attempt to calm the storm by pruning and cutting back in many important areas of their company. However, a company can do only so much slicing before the pain exceeds the gain.

In examining this book's previous text and cases we find two major points: Many sicknesses and maladies striking companies have common symptoms, and secondly, many sicknesses and maladies striking companies also DO NOT have common symptoms. What is good for one patient is not necessarily what another patient needs.

And from a global prospective, turnarounds in China and Russia are going to be much different than in other countries. They have thousands of state-owned enterprises that will have to be turned around or closed. Regionally too, restructuring and change will differ, as in the Asia Pacific region versus the Americas' region, for example.

But from the mouths of the CEOs, board members, shareholders, and workers there is a unanimous agreement that a turnaround expert is usually needed no matter where or when.

Studying the company of Toyota, Japan, one sees such success in other companies from Singapore to Brasil—companies large and small that have struggled and survived. And like Toyota, they have planned ahead. Founding a school for young people to groom the students to be Toyota workers and executives, is an example of strong planning for a healthy company's future. And that type of planning, it is hoped, could be the final phase of any company's successful turnaround.

Part I presented to you the essentials of corporate turnarounds from a global perspective, and also brief examples of cases and analysis.

In Part II the emphasis will be on companies, again from different countries, however, in a more detailed analysis. In both Parts the turnaround principles may apply to both small or large companies, and healthy as well as sick companies.

PART II

Case Studies and Turnaround Tools

Rebuilding trust of investors, employees, customers, and lenders

In Part I of this book we described the environment of companies either in need of recovery or seeking to better their performance and the help that they needed. In this part we will examine certain cases that illustrate that a turnaround can be a controllable crisis.

1. There is a significant difference today in Asian turnarounds than before, and that is the overwhelming rate of speed in which it is now occurring. Turnaround means a concerted top down effort, through central planning, to overcome negative elements of the past, adapting to a changing environment with the will to endure the painful effects of massive change.

   For instance, WNS a Mumbai based outsourcer wasn't alone in being affected by the sub prime problems in August 2007. Even before the actual arrival of the problem the company had declared its investors that their clients were reducing their loans. They tried to keep a balance by reducing the revenues and tried collecting payments much faster as compared to their usual decided period which saved them from mishap.

2. A Hong Kong listed company, managed by the major shareholder, the chairman, and his family was initially a garment manufacturer, they expanded into other related businesses and one not so related—property management ventures in the PRC. Although the garment business grew over the years as their core business, the management involved members of the family who were inexperienced, particularly in accounting and financial management.

The chairman and another member of the company had good contacts in the new project area, but the development team was without property development experience. The company took on a major office and residential project, however, as they were beginning the development the property values in the site areas fell, which lessened the security values on the property held by their bankers. In addition, the company faced stiff competition in its core business, the garment industry, and cash flow forced the company to go to its financial limits, worrying the bankers more. An assessment of the company's health situation was made, and these are the findings: Poor management by family members destroyed the formal reporting structure and this needed to be rehabilitated. International trade expertise was needed to keep the textile products competitive in a highly global competitive business. These errors caused many competent managers to leave. Management was resistant to change. The company's information processes and accounting systems were sub-standard. There were no management accounts or forecasts. Finally, there was a total lack of management of stock, inventory and obsolescence ratings.

For a successful turnaround the following changes were required:

Restoration of the information systems and monitoring to achieve proper management control; competent and professional management; a clear marketing strategy focusing on the competitive advantage of the company's core businesses; reduction of operating costs to a level that will work for the longer term. A capital structure needed to be implemented that would meet the future requirements of the business. The operating and other efficiencies tended to go along with production planning, machine production and updated technology. Equally Important was the need to rid themselves of non-core businesses by selling them off and improving their cash flow. And as we have stated earlier in this book there must be a correct mix of professional turnaround advice and that often extends beyond accountants and lawyers. There will have to be compromises as the turnaround team moves the recovery along[1].

3. It is quite a different story with another Chinese company: State-run <u>Shanghai Automotive Industry Corp</u>. began as a manufacturer of farm tractors, and since 1984 has not remained stagnant: it has grown by using and promoting government-negotiated joint venture agreements working with its core products with Volkswagen and General Motors. It plans to expand greatly in the next decade with the goal of becoming one of the world's six largest automakers by 2020--being up there with GM, Toyota, Ford, Daimler Chrysler and Volkswagen. It has also taken a stake in a Korean company Ssangyong Motor, and in 2004 boldly tried to buy the British Group, ending up with two Rover Models it now sells under its own brand.

The success of growth and not staying flat by Shanghai Automotive now puts them in an excellent position to move on the marketing front. A non-performing company often has to pass up such opportunities[2].

For example, China's own domestic market for their products is in rapid growth. They are now in a position to make the domestic market their growth. Their Chairman Hu Maoyuan indicated in 2006 that their goal for 2010 is to be manufacturing two million vehicles, with their own first hitting the streets in 2007. What will they do with all those vehicles, you ask? Well, in China today, the income is rising in many parts and there are estimated to be only 8 vehicles per one thousand of population, whereas in Japan, for example, the number is 502 vehicles per one thousand people.

And the don't-rest-upon-your-laurels example of Shanghai Automotive is true with many other companies in Asia such as Lenovo, Samsung, and Toyota. With overseas investment restrictions expected to be lifted in China, many companies in either growth or turnaround there will have an option of not only creating and borrowing, but also buying. From the cases to date it is clear that Chinese based and run companies, and perhaps most Asian companies, plan longer term growth compared to the West: centuries have taught the Chinese people to be patient and not be overly governed by the quarterly earnings crunch. In planning for a turnaround and recovery this factor is most important.

4. Airlines in recent years have been one of the more active participants in turnaround business. Few have escaped making major changes in their operation. The ones that avoided bankruptcy and made the necessary operational or marketing changes early are ahead of the field today. An example is <u>Qantas Airways</u> in Australia. The Qantas case was touched on earlier in this book. After struggling in recent years with deficits this fine airline has recently taken the option that is becoming more available to companies in the ASEAN area—the infusion of capital by a private equity investment firm. We will discuss the private equity option here.

In the past years, private equity firms have met with some resistance in both Europe and Asia and have not been a turnaround option. This has been true due to a national sentiment against foreign companies coming in and investing, and in some cases taking control of a company, or worse simply buying into a company for tax reasons or to sell or take it public to a listed company in three to five years. In the process, the customers, the stakeholders, and the employees have taken last place and in other cases the company is moved from the sick ward to the morgue. This is changing. The private equity firm that invested in Qantas Airways had the experience of turning around another major airline and recovering it to solid status (Continental Airlines) before they invested in Qantas. They also had a team that was experienced in Airline operations and the airline industry.

Besides the Qantas example, a private equity firm invested over US$1billion this year into hospitals in Singapore and Malaysia, a department store in Australia, a natural gas producer in China, and insurance companies in Taiwan and India. The amount they have earmarked for Asia next year is estimated to be many times more, perhaps 4 billion US dollars. For turnaround options these firms have clearly changed their approach with Asian companies, and are recovering from the bad reputation they received in Asia during the "economic crisis" in the late 1990s. It is estimated that these firms have committed US$28.9 billion through the first nine months of 2006 in Asian companies outside of Japan[3].

5. But the turnaround field does not just limit itself to problems with lessening sales or obsolete product/service, or weakened cash flow, a multi-disciplinary approach has to be taken as well. Here are some examples:

-After a company's operational and financial audit by outside professionals, it was discovered there was an ongoing theft in the company. It was difficult to discover as it was as hidden as in the Enron Energy Company case, Supra. The company was a large machining house and it took walk-around management to discover and eliminate the problems, in addition a change of job descriptions and implementation of scrupulous financial standards completed the turnaround.

-In another manufacturing company in Asia the company's banker was difficult and very anxious to protect its security interests first and in court. Loan extensions were needed to ease cash flow and not sink the entire boat. The solution came in both technical and design management of products, concessions from vendors and taxation authorities, and a refinanced loan with another bank.

-A major technology manufacturer in the global market made the final turn in its turnaround in 2006. It set a goal of growing 6% a year, and surpassed that goal in the last year. The general rule has been that large company's turnaround is slower than smaller companies because the smaller company is more nimble and less bureaucratic. And that was initially true as the company started out on its recovery. It reduced its payroll by 15,000 employees around the world and cut its expenses drastically to become more efficient, learning that cost-cutting improves the bottom line faster than the top line.

One of the options in the turnaround process was to acquire other companies and diversify their product offerings. They instead decided that it was too distracting and what they had to do was add revenue by growing from within. This is often the slow way of growth, but in many cases successful. The company is enhancing its core business of selling and designing printers as they provide nearly one-half of all printers sold throughout the globe, but also designing new products and services such as in-store printing kiosks, digital prints online, and providing major backstop photo printing operations for major retailers.

In the last year they have offered low-cost corporate data centers. Their consumer electronics lines are considered more risky. It appears they have made the right decisions from seeing their financial reports of 2006.

-Financial crises come and go, but when they come, like a sickness or disease the diagnosis is often masked as to the cause of the patient's malady: so with a company. In the midst of globalization, organizational factors and the Asian financial crisis of the late nineties, one of China's leading electronics firms was forced to develop a turnaround program as it was on the edge of bankruptcy. The recovery success of Huajing Electronics Group Corporation shows how recognizing the importance of the Chinese culture and a new program of retraining in entrepreneurial know-how saved the company and turned it into a vibrant competitor in the international and domestic marketplace. Their path to competing in emerging markets facing globalization is an example to other Asia firms doing so. The key points for their transformation facing challenging circumstances are as follows:

1. Huajing Electronics Group Corp., like other Chinese companies traditionally, relied upon savings capital for operational capital to generate growth. Facing losses, the company moved beyond this traditional form of financial resources to more of a type of financing prominent in the East Asian companies.

2. They changed their operational strategy to moving beyond only product manufacturing to also include product development.

3. The company pulled back from low-margin, loss-making business lines.

4. They developed their own in-house skills by investing in training. This allowed them to make technology transfer deals that could be utilized fully.

This example shows that companies in China can be unique and not comparable in terms of turnaround to the western companies in certain ways: Huajing Electronics had to overcome many traditional and cultural ways of doing business. Companies that have state supported help sometimes are dull on their entrepreneurial capabilities. However the state help can be commendable, because compared to the state paying huge sums of social benefits to the unemployed, the seriously sick patients, it is well recognized that several milligrams of prevention is worth a great deal more than several grams of treatment.

-While technology transfer agreements are a way to forge ahead in the marketplace of an industry, particularly in technological transfer, the newly acquired transfer often does not include sufficient training. This has been a major problem because most domestic firms have few in-house experienced personnel for training. With the new technology they acquire and in several turnaround cases in the Asia Pacific area this has meant that after the transfer the continuous process of product design and development using the new technology is not efficient and considerable time and capital are lost. This is changing as Newly Industrialized Countries (NIC) like Singapore, Taiwan, and South Korea, have developed competitive Asian positions by emphasizing proper training and know-how: best made in the beginning than during a loss and recovery phase.

-Another aspect that resembles an almost uncontrollable force, as do acts of nature, are the energy and oil prices: and this has resulted in tremendous costs pressures in recent times for all airlines. Korean Air Co., South Korea's top airline has finally emerged into the profit picture at the end of 2006, and suggests their turnaround has been due to: lower fuel costs, but also their route expansions in emerging markets, including China. They are one of the world's major air freight carriers, whose sales depend upon the international economy. They are expanding this successful cargo business by forming a joint venture with a Chinese company to service the growing Chinese air cargo market: an example of how a downside may be positive and lead to new markets, new products, and new partners.

-Taiwan companies have been the leading producers of supporting components to the world's well known companies with globally recognized brands, particularly in the manufacturing areas of LCD monitors, PC notebooks, and PDAs. The profits, however, on these products that are branded in the customer name have been drastically falling. Companies in this landscape in Taiwan are faced with threatening losses. Competitively, they cannot demand more for their product from their customers. If they attempted to establish their own brands, which would be a turnaround program, they would have to be very careful not to antagonize their core customers by competing against them. It is very difficult to solve this problem and it can very soon lead to major business failures if not turned around for a company.

One Taiwanese company that is trying to turn this squeeze position around has this solution that it hopes will work: They purchased a globally recognized brand named product (Siemens) with the right to use the major brand name for a period of years (5) while they (BenQ's), and the product they purchased rights to is not in direct competition with their core customers' products of which they provide. Other Taiwan companies are beginning to follow a similar program out of the profit squeeze while they still can, for example TVP, which purchased part of the Netherlands's Philips Company's computer display business, making TVP the largest computer display manufacturer in the global market. These preventive measures it is hoped will bring success and endorse principle of not waiting until the temperature rises and the blood pressure falls[4].

-Examples of company growth decisions and plans can be valuable for guides in what a company can do when it is in a less fortunate position. Studying how healthy companies continue to grow is essential in strategic turnaround planning. Looking at Mitac International, one of the larger computer manufacturers in Taiwan, for example, they have planned to purchase a smaller software company that will help them build up their online distribution system of their products allowing them to sell in new markets like India and Ireland. We have touched upon this point earlier in this book, pointing out the need of having the proper technology to attract orders, using that technology from new customers and new markets. Certainly this should be a tool on any turnaround team's workbench[5].

-Cutting off credit to a business is like ending blood flow to an organism. Once a bank acts in this way, the expectation is the company will go under. What can be done? A middle sized family owned Tool Company had an answer, but it took nearly three years to recover. The bank's final advice was a suggestion to the CEO to retain an accountant who specialized in turnarounds. He sold some of the company land to pay for the help, which turned out to be a good investment. Other than that he started taking anti-depressant medication, which his doctor ordered.

After a walk through the shop and a review of the books it showed the company was facing a complete meltdown. But the staff was skilled, the CEO was willing to make whatever changes were needed, the customers were always treated well and were loyal to the company, and the plant had good equipment. The expert believed there was hope. This was all laid out in a new proposal to the bank that relented foreclosure a bit. "If our bank forecloses now or in 30 days it won't make much of a difference," the loan officer concluded.

Getting to work quickly, the CEO, staff and the turnaround expert, followed up on the findings:

-A cost analysis had showed that while the machines were running, many orders were not particularly profitable. "Our company must not chase revenues and forget about profits," was written on the sales desk bulletin board and it became the gist of a number of meetings with employees. As a result, the team agreed to raise some prices and drop one large customer that was not profitable enough.

-To raise cash, they contacted their remaining good customers and the largest supplier. The goal was to get these customers to pay more quickly while the supplier was asked to increase the credit level. On the supply end, the steel company agreed to let the company have $2 worth of product for each $1 paid, up too a given limit, and not charge interest on any bill less than 70 days old. Nearly three years later they were back in the black and on good terms with the bank. And the CEO no longer requires the medication.

-A Malaysian company decided they needed completely new management. The new management replaced old staff with new ones to revamp the company and take corrective measures before it was too late. The new management found that the machinery needed upgrading and the product mix improved. Once this was done the company has seen increasing sales volume and after posting a net loss in 2006 expects to be in the black in 2007. An emphasis was placed on better quality products, and this attracted several multi-national corporations to boost sales volume. In addition they upgraded one of their plants making their core product powder-free gloves for the healthcare and medical industries[6].

Examples herein have included a number of large companies, but bigger is certainly not necessarily better[7].Nimbleness and flexibility to recover are more important.

 -Although patients have often similarities in condition, in the medical environment the proper treatment is often in the details of the difference. In companies the same applies. What is good for one may not be the proper medicine for the other. It has been estimated that seventy percent of change programs fail. A set program that works on one may fail on the next. This is the bad news part. As the downturn becomes worse for the patient or the company--the surgery needed becomes more complex and riskier.

A change management firm studied 21 of the most remarkable transformation stories of recent years and discovered in their report of 2002 that four principles underpinned the success of each one of those companies. Although the principles are easy to write they are not easy to achieve:

- *Set high standards and lead by example.*

- *Put the right managers in place and give them real power.*

- *Focus on results, not on an elaborate change process.*

120

- *Do it quickly—tackle issues in parallel not in sequence[8].*

The conclusion of this study conforms to other studies and they advise that the implementation of these four points is not easy. In order to put the right managers in place and give them real power it may take an entire change of management. Then keeping a clear view of the path the company must take is critical, and some incentives, such as small bonuses to the employees for outstanding performances are one of the better investments. An example cited is Continental Airlines that made a tough turnaround in difficult market and industry times. They provided employees incentives linked to short-term and clearly identified goals such as their on-time bonus of $65 or $100 a month. The Bain study also indicated that the turnaround programs that work are usually completed in less than three years. One other company mentioned in the study notes was Optus Communications a telecommunications firm in Australia. In the late nineties the company faced problems of before-tax losses, cash squeezes, the end of Australia's telephone duopoly, and a revolving door to the CEO's office. The company came within an inch of liquidating.

Optus's successful turnaround started after they replaced the CEO and CFO and installed an entirely new management team for fresh blood, without the anchors of doing things the same as before or holding on to positions that needed revamped. They brought the cash flow shortage under control, and a number of other measures of efficiency then implemented a long delayed IPO. In 2001 it was purchased by Singapore Telecom for twice the IPO price.

Endnotes for Section:

1 *Zelium International Ltd. MBA Notes (2006)*

2 *Far Eastern Economic Review,* Ellis & Gadish. 07/07/06

3 *"The Biggest Private Equity Firms Turn Their Focus To Asia"* NYT 12/27/06

4 *Time,* Asia Edition, M. Schuman-Taipei. 12/29/06
What additional points would you add to the list as important?

5 *Mitac sees a turnaround as sales surge,* Taipei Times, Nystedt. 6/15/02

6 *APLI expects turnaround in FY07,* The Edge Daily, Gan Yen Kuan 12/30/06

7 *Corporate Suicide; Getting Bigger Instead of Better,* Dr. Mike Teng, author of a best – selling business book, Corporate Turnaround: Nursing a Sick Company back to Health

8 *Making Change Stick,* Bain & Company, Stan Pace/Paul Rogers 5/1/02

The following are some questions pertaining to the above case studies:

- In the Hong Kong garment case: textile manufacturing worldwide faced strong competition from very low paid wage companies in other countries. Should the company have made some management decisions before feeling confident about their core industry and before trying a new industry? What particular management positions did they seem to need? Would the company have possibly succeeded better with some fresh and experienced management?

- Also in the Hong Kong case, should they have concentrated more on creating a better core product in view of international competition, rather than diversify? One suggestion that was made to them by their bank was that they should have an experienced international competition analysis before they did anything. Do you agree? Explain.

- If you were on a turnaround team helping a family owned company, what special factors might you have to deal with that would not be present in non-family owned companies? Would your answer be different whether the family owned company was doing business internationally or just domestically?

- Why is it that Asian companies such as the Shanghai Automotive Corp., do so well in improving by using alliances with other companies so successfully? Alliances that allow for teamwork between two companies seem to work well in the Asia business culture. Why?

- Why are alliances so popular in countries such as China?

- Has Qantas Airlines of Australia accepted only a short term solution to their operational and cash flow problems by agreeing to a large, but not controlling investment by a foreign private equity firm? What are their risks?

- Do private equity firms that seem to be pouring into the ASEAN market area in all industries offer a new source of turnaround relief capital to ailing and sick companies or are some of them scalpers that snap up corporate corpses? Please discuss.

- There are many causes of a company downturn. In the case where theft was discovered involving millions of US dollars, it was in a U.S. company (Enron) where the prevailing view and law is minimum government interference of business? How much should the government of a country police its companies?

- It is said that new product defines a company. How did an Asian manufacturing company in need of a turnaround solve its product and banker problem?

- What steps did a major worldwide technology manufacturer of printers and other PC related products take to change course from losing operations to profitability once again?

- When a company has as its "partner" a government, what changes can take place in the favor of the company in the competitive marketplace, and how does it change for the better, such as in Huajing Electronics Group of China?

- While having the government as a partner may cause certain changes in a company compared to companies that do not have such an "advantage," what negative forces can such assistance bring? Please discuss.

- A considerable amount of developing business in many countries is due to technology transfer, and this promotes advances for companies that by using it can conserve considerable time, cash, and allows them to hit the competitive market quickly. However, in the technology case cited, what has been the downside to technology transfer that has led some companies into trouble?

- There are controllable and uncontrollable forces in doing business. We cannot manage earthquakes, fires, political instability, tsunamis, and Acts of God as defined in the international maritime laws. Surviving them is the first order. It is debatable if energy and fuel is controllable or not—recently it seems as if it is not controllable. This strikes good companies, and it struck Korean Air, one of the largest cargo carriers in the world as it did many airlines. Comment on the way Korea Air has worked to turnaround by trying some new operations.

- As computer hardware prices sink, so do the prices paid to the makers of the component parts and the computers and gear. What tools are some Taiwanese companies using to survive this squeeze?

- The family-owned tool company faced a cutoff of credit from their bank. What measures did the CEO and owner of the company take to recover?

- An example of the positive results of fresh management is noted in the medical and health products supplier case from Malaysia. How did new management make the difference in that case?

- Please comment on the "Bigger is not necessarily better" concept and why a smaller company may be in a much better position to recover faster from the financial and operational doldrums? Would your answer change if the company is trading internationally?

- Considering the four points of the study of turnaround companies, what additional points would you add to the list as important?

PART III. SOLUTIONS FOR TURNAROUND

For both sick and healthy companies, it is found that an early diagnosis and treatment are always the best counsel.

- We reviewed two family owned companies that at one time were profitable with their core products. One in Asia and the other a tool company in the West. Both waited until they were on the edge of bankruptcy to change. Many waiting that long would not make it. Family owned businesses have many advantages, but like in all cases they must be examined differently because of the way decisions are made. This can lead to incompetent management because of the tendency to promote family members whether they are competent or not, and the tendency to avoid strict financial and accounting rules and operation. Before long the inefficiency of these factors take their toll on the company.

The first step in their turnarounds was to cut non-essential costs. Asian company outside management was brought in and decisions were made to eliminate a distracting and cash draining new business venture of real estate development when the core business was textiles. Outside counsel was obtained as well and the problem identified by the astute professional, showed the company to be in worse shape than it had originally thought it was. With a plan of recovery, the bank that was ready to call it quits reconsidered and agreed to stick with the company for a short time. What did they have to lose by waiting? They asked themselves. And the answer was nothing. But it wouldn't have

126

happened unless the recovery team, the CEO and the expert had mapped out a path out of the woods that convinced the bank the tool company could return to profitability.

The plan they mapped out was one that involved their major creditor—their supplier of raw materials—obtaining more time to pay accounts payable, and with their customers: paying accounts receivable earlier. And all this took considerable time, face to face time—communications at the most direct levels.

- A Chinese automotive company was helped by being a state assisted company. However, it was also hampered by the state controls that limited foreign investment as an option of help that it could not take advantage of. Similar to what many Asian companies have done, this automotive company formed alliances and joint ventures, particularly with two key customers GM and Volkswagen. This was the major tool to its recovery. Perhaps it is the culture of certain Asian companies and countries that bolsters the ability to cooperate and work as a team with outsiders. There have been many joint ventures and alliances that have not worked so well in the West.

We reviewed other companies that choose the same tools for recovery. Kia Motors was the other example, when it teamed up with Hyundai and thereafter survived from a financial collapse through Hyundai's change management that replaced the Kia management.

When Caterpillar and Matsushita joined hands in working together they regained market share after a downward spiral against the major competitor Komatsu. Dell computers did not expend huge sums of capital to build plants to increase their product line by developing strong relationships with Fuji Xerox, Samsung, Lexmark, and Kodak. This helped Dell to compete against giants that could bury Dell in computers and peripheral equipment. The motto of let the one who makes it best—do it, and not try to imitate and fail has worked for Dell and many others.

This method of turnaround and growth, by forming alliances and joint ventures has been a critical tool in turnaround essentials and solutions. The plan was followed when two strong companies partnered in recent years: Pepsi Cola and Starbucks. Starbucks did not learn the beverage business and Pepsi did not learn the coffee business. Neither one had to invest in expensive experts to invest in another market—they each had a partner that would competitively do that.

- The Malaysian medical products manufacturer we discussed used the tool of change of management to immediately move the company out of a staid position. This is not always true that current management needs to be replaced. But if it is warranted it must be tried, and here it worked: The equipment was updated and the product mix changed. In this case it was assessed early as the present management would not be able to do the job. The company returned to health.

- The airline turnaround cases that we've examined all share a common factor in their decline of profits in recent years, and that is the price of fuel—their energy costs: Qantas, Malaysia Airlines, Northwest, and Continental. The same with the Asian Financial Crisis of the late nineties: a common factor for loss of growth or profit was the crisis and not necessarily management or product. In such matters of serious impact there are companies that make it and some which do not. The crisis masks some of the real reasons. And in other cases it is the booster that instigates the company to change, such as Singapore Airlines has done with a level of service to customers unequaled in the industry.

-       One solution tool suggested by Jack Welch, the former CEO of General Electric was that the turnaround and change management program must have flexibility built into it. Although clear-cut goals are essential, the path to arrive there may have to be tuned on the journey to corporate health. In the next Part, Part IV, the cases and analysis will illustrate challenges in the world of turnarounds.

PART IV. BOOMERANGS IN THE BUSINESS WORLD

1. People and Ethics Matter

A saying that has survived the ages is "What goes around comes around." Some souls appear to have escaped this sign on life's wall. But it can be argued that in the short life people have on this planet that if they use that life for cheating, bullying, or mistreating others they will become diseased in some phase of their cycle. The former CEO of Enron suffered a fatal heat attack during his first month in prison and subsequently died a few months later. Are the millions that he stole and the thousands he caused the loss of jobs worth it?

Although applicable to many situations, it certainly applies to business, and particularly to a business that is in a troubled state of affairs. Businesses will reap, as people will what they sow.

When the amazing Richard Branson was interviewed on keys for success of Virgin Airlines, he replied: "I'm absolutely certain that it is a question of the kind of people you have; the way you motivate your people. I'm sure that is what makes a company successful. If you can motivate your people you can get through bad times, and you can enjoy the good times together. If you fail to motivate your people, your company is doomed not to perform well. I find that I spend a lot of time trying to concentrate on motivating.

As was stated earlier in this book, the gremlins that are not visible on the financial papers of a company are like unseen viruses and bacteria—they can be fatal to the health of the company. Often, this has been proven true as the health of the company is diagnosed and treated. Each country has its own standards on accounting and even in the west the standards differ, for example, between the UK and the U.S. It is true also in Asia. The ugliest effect of this kind of chicanery is its impact on those who rely on a company for their own and their families' livelihood, and the investors who have often trusted their hard-earned savings over many years with a company's management.

2. The Positive Side of What Is Not On A Balance Sheet—Human Capital

If there is a any great secret of success in life
it lies in the ability to put one self in another's
place and see things from another's point of view
as if it were your own.
-Henry Ford

There are positive forces not shown on the balance or financial sheets of a company as well: The assets Mr. Branson of Virgin group referred to—the company employees. When a company is sick, employees make the difference in success if they have leadership and a mission they believe in. Good employees, well motivated, have the ability to take a boomerang from competitions and flip it back: restoring the company through dedication and work. There are many examples of this. Harley-Davidson Motorcycle Company was facing bankruptcy just when motorcycles were becoming popular with different age groups again. The factory faced closure. Through the hard work of the company employees who were dedicated and motivated to keep the low throated Harley roaring on the streets of the world a restoration was begun. Employees worked long hours and many months without pay. Management communicated with them on a weekly basis, having personal picnics where the company made their work teamwork. And management mixed socially with the employees at their factory picnics, not through some third party such as E-mail, but face to face, handshake to handshake, and ear to ear. When the company finally made its turnaround, they did as Mr. Branson suggested: ". . . celebrate their success together." The "extra" that is so essential. And it doesn't appear anywhere on the financial papers that a company files.

A CEO of one of the largest banking services in the world enjoys his lunches in different restaurants, as many of us do. She also writes food review columns of her chosen restaurants when her CEO duties allow her. She started as a low paying secretary in the company, working her way through college. The first thing she looks for in a restaurant is something of a surprise. Her experience coming up the management ladder gives a clue: Do the restaurant employees seem to be enjoying their work in this restaurant? This is a mainstay in her popular restaurant reviews. If a restaurant's management is cheating or abusing their employees, she makes it known, and will never lunch there again. It is the people thing she is examining. Without this element the greatest food in the world is tasteless.

The spirit and passion of a company do not seep through the walls accidentally: spirit and passion for making the company a success is the responsibility of management. If it isn't, then why hire them? If management cannot instill a force of passion and spirit for the company they should find other work—they don't belong in management. They wouldn't be hired by Richard Branson (Virgin) or Jack Welch (GE) or if they accidentally were they would be terminated before they suck in the passion of the company dry because of their own lack of talent for the job or selfishness or some other leadership weaknesses. This is why there is often a change in management during a turnaround. They may still be contagious with their disease, so why keep them? Spirit and passion—the enthusiasm and fuel that a healthy company runs on is hard to measure in numbers. Social engineers have been trying for centuries. Each year there are new gimmicks that both the educational industry and academics have announced claiming success in the "business" of human prediction. Mostly they have failed.

Spirit and passion are wonderful magic forces where life stumps technology.

For an example of "what goes around comes around," the history of Sam Walton, the founder of Wal-Mart provides a picture. He took five hours at a shareholders meeting to individually thank his then four thousand excellent performing staff. Afterwards, he invited them all to his home.

In a short poll taken in 2006 of key production people in listed companies, it was determined that none of these key personnel had ever met their CEO or upper management. If the CEO and management faced a deadly disease called low sales and low cash flow, would these workers be inclined to work without pay for people they had never met? Hardly.

There were some relevant findings made that illustrate the above point further: In 1978, on average, book value represented 95% of market value for a company, while 10 years later it was 28%. Today, it is estimated that 80% of stock value is driven from assets that do *not* (emphasis added) appear on balance sheets, assets like people, brands, knowledge, and relationships.

It is the wrong emphasis to place on a company, particularly when it is sick, to quack into the wind with strategies and resolutions when you do not have the right people doing the job. To make a turnaround compete successfully people are needed to perform successfully on an internal company level.

People often marvel at Bill Gates, Jr. the founder of Microsoft and describe him as either rich or giving away a lot of his billions. He is described as impatient. He is that. But he is usually impatient with sloppiness. If the essentials of a meeting cannot be explained in thirty minutes or reduced to notes on a 3 X 5 card (inches)—he's gone. He is an example of innovation. He is an example for his employees many of whom are dedicated and passionate about the success of their company. When most heads were turned in the late seventies to designing the big iron of computing, he concentrated on the nervous system of computing—software. When the big opportunity came with IBM he was ready: "Let them do the hardware thing and I'll do the software," he must have thought.

But the other side of Bill's story is that money never was his motivation. He came from a family of considerable dedication to helping their fellow human beings—this was how he was raised and how he is now living his life. Mother, Mary, gave hours of her time and talent to education and solving the needs of those who were without. Bill's father was one of Seattle's finest lawyers and helped his community in many ways. When Bill became bored with college and cycled up the driveway, this is the kind of home he returned to. If his dear mother then said to herself, "I don't know what is going to happen with that boy," no one would blame her. What goes around comes around. Gates, the younger, saw the big picture.

Another aspect that the figures don't show is companies that aren't feeling well and are going to the doctor *before* the symptoms spell real trouble and maybe hospitalization. CEO turnover has skyrocketed in the past six years. In just 2005 alone, in the U.S. 1,322

Chief Executives stepped down. According to Challenger, Gray & Christmas, a premier outplacement organization, an average of six CEOs retire or step down each day of significant listed companies. In 2006 this number rose by 11%. When this occurs and trouble is common, many companies are turning to former CEOs with experience.

Age is less important—ability, aptitude, and experience is in demand. The cliff of retirement is no longer 65. Companies looking for a helmsman are less hampered by age. This has been the case with many major players in the U.S: Apple Computer, Kraft, Boeing, Delta Air Lines, Honeywell International, Corning, Dow Chemical and Lucent Technologies. All these companies moved before they had to go to the hospital. They moved to leadership with experience. And as it turned out their moves made successful turnaround boomerangs possible.

An article in the *Financial Times* in November of 2006 indicated that the mid-sized company stocks are outperforming the mega-mega company stocks when one examines the top of the FTSE 100. One of the reasons offered were large companies do not have the option that mid-size companies have in the sizzling mergers and acquisitions arena. It is this arena that offers companies one turnaround option in times of trouble. Even pension funds seem to be selling out of the mega cap stocks and then reinvesting their monies in areas such as private equity, which then recycles the money back into the smaller company market.

But as we have stated earlier, if the mergers and acquisitions sizzle might help, it also can sure be a mess. The examples of failures of M&As as a reliable option for turnaround and change are numerous: "Neither Glaxo's merger with Smith Kline nor Vodafone's acquisition of Mannesmann has delivered value for shareholders of those companies," reported the *Financial Times*. The article lists other factors that may have made these companies big but they are not so beautiful. Some may be controllable and some may not. However, an investor change of mindset is occurring, and this may prompt an early call to their doctors.

We have suggested many options in restructuring in the turnaround process in this book. No one formula is going to fit each patient. A World Bank quote from the *Asian Development Review, Vol. 23 (2006)* goes as follows:

> *There is no universal set of rules . . .we need to get away*
> *from formulae and the search for the elusive "best practices".*
> *. . . and rely on deeper economic analysis to identify the*
> *binding constraints of growth . . . .*

And by the Inter-American Development Bank (2005, 3):

> *Whatever the policy area, there is no single formula*
> *applicable to all circumstances: policies' effectiveness*
> *depends upon the manner in which they are discussed,*
> *approved, and implemented . . . . A strictly technocratic*
> *approach toward policy making and change management*
> *shortchanges these steps.*

Rules of thumb depend upon many other factors to be in place.

3. Big Is Not Necessarily Beautiful

The middle market for investors is made up of smaller, usually more recent enterprises. Many are under capitalized. Banks often are not their first line of helpful credit. In this state, these companies, many with great promise, are far from immune from the germs of slowdown. If banks do make a loan they often take only a credit review once a year.

These companies in the middle market segment require more frequent monitoring to keep healthy. In many countries and in the U.S. these smaller companies offer the most new jobs. From 1970 to 2000, for example, the *Fortune 500* companies cut 4 million jobs in the U.S. alone, while the smaller new companies created new positions—more jobs than were cut by the big fellows.

It is understood that there has been a rise in human capital as an element in valuing a company. This is one reason cited for going on to graduate school for those planning management careers. Growth financing looks first at helping companies that are smaller and have clearly performing management. In a turnaround condition these companies have a better chance of obtaining capital at a very critical time in their operations.

In terms of obtaining needed capital from banks the smaller company is, however, often rated too low and the mega companies, too high, out of inertia. The credit ratings during turnaround phases don't always reflect the smaller company's true picture and value. The smaller companies, investors have agreed, when examined carefully beyond the credit ratings, and with good monitoring and nurturing can be very profitable. Change management experts have found that although mid-sized companies are often headed by very knowledgeable leaders as to their products and industry, they are not so knowledgeable on financial matters. This calls for change management experts to nurture the company in its recovery phase and not just check figures on a regular basis. This is true for a number of reasons, but essentially it is true because human capital is the key to a recovery. It is the change management person's duty to educate management on financial markets. An unfortunate truth is that the best time to finance is when you don't need the money. In summary, it certainly does not take size for success and the current stock market is reflecting that, showing a trend for more faith in the smaller companies, which are often more flexible and can move faster when the storm clouds appear on the horizon.

In considering the changes that will affect the social-psychological health of an organization large or small, given the uncertainty that change clouds bring with them, it is a given that trust and work satisfaction will be negatively affected. However, in companies where these changes took place and the managers and supervisors directly helped and listened to the employees affected, there was a considerable positive difference. When employees ride through the following thorny bushes their trust is affected whether they end up with a job or not:

-Cost cutting by downsizing

-Reorganizing the divisions

-Streamlining operations

-Closing down unprofitable cost centres

The research has shown that trust fades first and is then closely followed by work satisfaction. But the plus side of all of this is it doesn't have to be that way. In talking to employees and managers it was found that positive relationships between the people, whether managers and employees, or just the employees themselves, can make a difference. If the managers and the supervisors listen and help the employees, that obstacle can be turned around. In other words, when the changes make a social impact, and they will, handling them properly is a key part of the mosaic of the turnaround.

The driver behind restructuring is, of course, that restructuring will improve cash flow and the business. The assumption is usually that the sickness was caused by inefficiency and managerial bungling. However the results of the change can show a mixed result: maybe it was the product etc. Not all turnarounds are going to be successful.

4. The Product Can Make or Break The Company

When a company needs a doctor, a turnaround expert, it has been found that in determining the diagnosis, the company products need to be examined as well. It is not enough that the company has an established Research and Development centre within the company or via collaboration with another company: it may not be producing new and profitable products. It may be only protecting the products that have already slowed down in sales—the core products for the company in the past. A good example of this is Microsoft. They invest six billion dollars a year in Research and Development. But 90% of this investment is devoted to improving their existing core product Windows. As a result, its return of investment is very poor.

But Apple did not sit on its laurels from the very successful launch of Mini iPod in 2005, their Research and Development centre kept working for new products and came up with the Nano iPod in 2006, which is an entirely new product—not just an improvement to their already successful core product. Nano iPod runs on a solid-state Flash memory instead of disk drive storage, allowing for a much smaller and more durable product. This move was considered very risky by the technology media. It is, however, a good example of top leadership: Steve Jobs has been consistent in repeatedly pushing his employees to take risks rather than fall into complacency (trying to protect the successful Mini).

Another example of the failure of executing on new products is Xerox: in the 1970s horse race of technology it was about as healthy a winner as a company can achieve. To continue their wins they set up a top notch R&D centre in California. This would normally be the right move if executed well. The purpose of the centre was to develop new products beyond the photocopier, and they did: the laser printer, the graphical interface, the mouse, and typography language among others. But none of these innovations entered the Xerox sales channels. Management was obviously still thinking copier thoughts. Other companies marketed those innovations: Canon and HP, the laser printers, Apple the graphics, and Adobe with typography. Mental block is not only a psychological condition it is also a corporate management malady. "If it runs, don't fix it" philosophy has stranded many a motorist on the road to success.

Much of what happens to top management is isolation, which is a similar virus that politicians seem to catch once they are elected. They are no longer mixing with their people, and the customers or employees. They read polls, and some may even have think tank groups: from this they erroneously believe they know what customers and employees want, need, or should have. With this kind of behavior, the winds of restructuring and trouble are starting to blow. One turnaround expert explained he could hear a need for change coming. When questioned, he explained that the noise he heard was the company's new corporate jet and that in his experience that would mean a crash sooner or later.

Yet, many company CEOs understand the principle of product development and take an active role in making sure the company does not sit on its hunches as a catcher does in a baseball game without end. An example was the former CEO of Medtronic, the well known medical pacemaker manufacturer. Medtronic reports that Medtronic's then CEO, Mr. Bill George, himself observed 1200 multi-hour surgeries during his highly successful 12 year tenure. He saw how the company products were used and how they could be better. He saw what frustrated physicians during the procedures and made copious notes on how the problem could be solved. The information came to him from what he observed, what he heard in offhand remarks at breakfasts with the surgeons, and the banter between the nurses and the doctors—first hand information. The information he has from hanging out at hospitals, chatting with physicians, and as a participant-observer. From a stumbling company of $750 million when he took over in 1989, he grew the company to $5 billion when he retired.

This is not a process that can be accomplished over the internet—vicariously. Not with the highly technical medical products that Medtronic manufactures that can mean life or death to patients. It is a process that requires an engagement of all senses, allowing valuable insights like breakthrough plastic container wraps that fully seal on contact and prevent ugly spills; diapers with non-plastic, cottony feel that make parents and babies happy, and colorful pop-up boxes of wipes.

The point is that product and design development should be an ongoing process such as it is at Toyota, Honda, Diebold, and Apple. A company can prevent deterioration by such policies. The best medicine for turnarounds is preventive medicine: never needing one. What is risky is when a company does not take risks for new products: They are in this slow moving game and the score is relatively even, the CEO and some of the board are out on the golf course—then a rival company hits an extra-base hit in the last innings, and they must jump from their paralysis to action or it will be too little, too late. That is risky. Thomas Friedman is the author of a number of books on globalization with his latest book entitled *The World Is Flat* wrote an article about oganizations led by the sense of a higher cause:

> *As globalization gives everyone the same information,*
> *resources, technology, and markets, an organization's ability*
> *to put these pieces together in the fastest and most innovative manner*
> *increasingly separates winners from losers in the global economy.*

Some companies caught in the spinning web of a downfall find the spin has hampered their innovative talents for better products just when they may need them. There has recently developed another option for companies—collaborating on product design and development with an offshore partner. This can save capital that would otherwise be invested in non-liquid research assets such as buildings and equipment, and expensively priced research and development personnel. While the U.S. remains the standard-bearer in terms of worldwide R&D, China is emerging as an R&D giant. That trend will continue, a report projects. We have moved as a world from the Arms Race (we hope), to the "Hands Race" and from there to a "Head and Brains Race," where nations measure their success through the development and application of technology. In the "Hands Race" it began as low labor costs, but it has evolved. And this is true in Asian countries, where the West is not only manufacturing at competitive costs, but also discovering new products at competitive prices. Statistics show that the U.S. is responsible for 32.4 percent of global R&D this year, compared to 13.4 percent for China. Those numbers were first and second, respectively, worldwide but represent a decline for the U.S. and an increase for China. The same trend will continue in 2007, according to the report, when the U.S. will be responsible for 31.9 percent of global R&D and China 14.8 percent.

Changed attitudes, direct government investments, liberalization of their economies, and an increased emphasis on developing a highly educated, technology-oriented population are some of the factors leading to the R&D growth in Asia. These also are reasons why industry from all over the world is changing the way it develops relationships with the R&D communities from these burgeoning countries. The first steps could be characterized as casual, "testing-the-waters" interactions that included preliminary contract research arrangements. These quickly have evolved into major investments in institution-building, the creation of subsidiary operations, and the development of a wide range of joint ventures.

"It is apparent that the modifications in the internal policies of East and South Asia, in particular, have had and will continue to have an influence on the amounts and patterns of R&D performance in the U.S. and other nations," says Tim Studt, editor of *R&D Magazine* and Duga's co-author on the report.

Outsourcing of R&D has been a growing trend and will continue to grow as long as the cost of doing business makes sense for U.S. companies, concludes the report. The lower costs in most areas, especially China and India, enhance the competitive position as compared to other (usually domestic) resources and lead to measures of higher productivity. When other advantages, such as enhanced global R&D infrastructure and improved support for other global operations, are considered, the value of outsourcing becomes apparent, says Duga.

5. **Intellectual Property**

Often forgotten in establishing the value of a company are its intellectual property assets: patents, copyrights, and trademarks. These valuable assets do not often appear on the financial statements, but if one is examining a manufacturing company, and preparing to help in a turnaround, the company's patent and trademark inventory are essential to appraise. In some companies, the most promising asset the company possesses is not the striking office or factory building, but the product idea behind their products—the patents and trademarks and copyrights. For an example, the following are patentable items:

- computer software and hardware;
- chemical formulas and processes;
- genetically engineered bacteria, plants, and animals;
- drugs;
- medical devices;
- furniture design;
- jewelry;
- fabrics and fabric design; and
- musical instruments.

Patent is often defined as follows: A patent is a right granted to an inventor by the government that permits the inventor to exclude others from making, selling or using the invention for a period of time. In the U.S. the U.S. Patent and Trademark Office grants patents for inventions that meet statutory criteria.

There are three different kinds of patents:

1. *Utility patents,* the most common type, are granted to new machines, chemicals, and processes.

2. *Design patents,* are granted to protect the unique appearance or design of manufactured objects, such as the surface ornamentation or overall design of the object.

3. *Plant patent,*. are granted for the invention and asexual reproduction of new and distinct plant varieties, including hybrids. Asexual reproduction means the plant is reproduced by means other than from seeds, such as by grafting or rooting of cuttings.

For an invention to qualify for a patent, it must be both "novel" and "non-obvious." An invention is novel if it is different from other similar inventions in one or more of its parts. It also must not have been publicly used, sold, or patented by another inventor within a year of the date the patent application was filed. This rule reflects the public policy favoring quick disclosure of technological progress. An invention is non-obvious if someone who is skilled in the field of the invention would consider the invention an unexpected or surprising development. [56]

---

[56] Findlaw, Thomson Publishing Ltd., 2007

An inventor applying for a utility patent also must prove that the invention is useful. The invention must have some beneficial use and must be operable. A machine that will not operate to perform its intended purpose would not be called useful, and therefore would not be granted a patent.

One of the dangers, if the turnaround for the company is not successful, is the intellectual property of the company may be sold off by the bankruptcy court. This is what we mean when we point out that if a turnaround does not succeed and bankruptcy occurs that the company loses control. Another danger to remember with intellectual property is that it is generally not self-protective. The holder of the patents must protect the rights to the property by agreements titled "Non-Disclosure Agreements." It is one of the first things an expert looks for in company records. Not being self-protective, intellectual property is lost too often by carelessness. It is also lost by going into markets in other countries without first knowing the intellectual property laws of the country. The Japanese patent law is quite different, for example, than the U.S. law on a few very important points.

Intellectual property law is a specialty like tax law, and highly trained and experienced legal counsel is always suggested in making operational decisions that involve the company's rights to intellectual properties.

Intellectual property rights can cause a great downturn and are the reason for many major medical companies to begin and enter the turnaround: Mr. Clark, 60 years old, has also raised morale among employees who have suffered from the company's Vioxx-related vilification. Shedding the aloof manner of many CEOs, he mingles with employees in the company cafeteria and holds meetings with groups of randomly selected employees once a month. During the meetings, Mr. Clark shares with employees a score card he keeps to chart progress toward the goals he has set, and encourages them to speak their minds. "The Merck culture had become too polite," he says.

Yet it isn't clear whether Merck's turnaround is sustainable, or how much Mr. Clark can claim credit for it. Merck's improved drug pipeline is chiefly the work of research head Peter Kim, and Merck's new drugs remain unlikely to make up for the huge revenue losses from old blockbusters going off patent.

The Merck's former top seller product, with a $4 billion-a-year cholesterol drug Zocor, lost patent protection in June, causing a plunge in the company's third-quarter profit. Fosamax, a $3 billion-a-year osteoporosis drug, will lose marketing exclusivity in 2008, followed by other big sellers, hypertension treatments.[57]

Most diseases, including cancer and heart problems are easier to cure if detected early. Similarly, most sick companies can be turned around if the problems are discovered early. In the Merck case above, the CEO began a program of reuniting the company and the employees for the tough days ahead when they were no longer world leaders in certain drugs. It was a fall from the top that he was getting ready for. And since a fall

---

[57] Wharton Business, 11/06

from the top can be started or resolved at the bottom, he immediately began working with the employees, opening communications and encouraging faster research for new drugs. In the pharmaceutical marketplace, depending upon the country the medical is launched, it can take as much as six years from the beta project to governmental approval. On the other hand, troubled companies often try to conceal their falling profits and what they see ahead as troubled times. They do this for the obvious reasons: creditors may stop their loans, suppliers may stop supplies, and they may start to lose the good employees which can rescue a company when in trouble. Like sick people, sick companies need urgent care, and good urgent care means seeking the care of specialists who have the experience and training to diagnosis the problems and sicknesses correctly, and to begin treatment with reconstruction measures and programs. Facing the reality of the situation is critical to the hope of recovery. Many companies have been destroyed by neglect. This should not happen when the CEO takes charge as the CEO has done in the Merck Company case.

That is why a regular health check should be the top priority for people as well as companies. A review of their intellectual property inventory will tell them the length of time they have on a monopoly for a particular product—a measure of the product's life cycle. Since the lead time in the drug manufacturing industry is so long this means that the concept for the new replacing product or products must begin soon after the initial product hits the market.

The real health of the company can be quickly damaged by irregularities in accounting that are deliberate such as in the recent cases of Enron and WorldCom. And these irregularities usually lead to other unhealthy conditions, such as a dangerously impaired CEO, criminal management teams, employee morale, and non-balance sheet and financial statement causes. A regular health check should include these areas for testing on a regular basis as well. Usually there are ample warning signs of trouble ahead. In a multi-billion dollar company the CEO was a drunk, and the company although showing accounting of huge profits to the stock market—showed no profit at all to the tax authorities. How can this be, you ask? The answer is that it can be and was the situation with Enron. And it is the situation with other companies as well. A regular health check would have discovered this if done objectively. And there were warning signs at Enron and World Com, but they were suppressed. Early diagnosis is always better than a post mortem[58].

On the economic front regular health check should provide management with a fitness level, that not only includes the tests we have discussed above, but also a serious review of leading economic indicators such as GDP growth, consumer confidence, industry specifics, and stock market growth. Political stability is also critical, but also on the industry front, a full picture of the company's profit and loss, business trends, consumer spending, the competition as well as product life cycle and intellectual property inventory.

From these health checks the company should determine if its problem is financial in nature, which could very well be a case of over-gearing and cash flow problems. Operational and control issues may be involved too, such as frauds, financial scandals, etc. These checks can prepare the top management for the exigencies such as a change of

[58] Dr. Michael Teng *Corporate Wellness: 101 Principles in Turnaround and Transformation, 2006*

political regime, government or terrorists attacks, etc. The company may have to employ

some form of financial re-engineering to resuscitate the company. If necessary, enlisting

the expertise of a turnaround professional can often save the ship from taking on further

water. Knowing the company is sinking is one thing, but doing something about it—

action—is critical, too.

6. Samples Concerning Bankruptcy, Accounting, and Financial Aspects

Examples covered:

- **Alpha Company-Textiles**
- **Beta Company-Computers**
- **Ford Motor Company-Vehicles/Downsizing**
- **Kaputsky Oil Company-Energy**
- **Financial Notes: China, India, and Silicon Valley**
- **Business Health Notes**

- **Alpha Company.*** The company (a psuedoname) was not the usual company

  coming to bankruptcy court. They were a worldwide leader in their industry of

  manufacturing textile products. They had successfully been doing business for

  200 years. The bankruptcy filing showed listed assets of almost $2.2 billion ($US)

  and debts of US$1.3 billion. The journey to bankruptcy court began first with an

  attempt internally to reorganize the company. The CEO agreed to resign. He was

  blamed for aggressive borrowing and spending he considered necessary over a

  period of four years (US$585 million). The second order of the day was reducing

  the debt.

- The board approved an eight point program. The Eight-Point Program was designed to provide dynamic flexibility within a strong framework of clear, measurable goals. The eight points were:

1) Rationalize Manufacturing: Alpha will conduct an intensified evaluation of its manufacturing process flow and capacity and how they relate to market demand. This should enable the Company to best rationalize manufacturing in bath products, sheeting and basic bedding areas and create a more flexible manufacturing environment. The USD125 million net restructuring charges will allow Alpha to consolidate manufacturing operations in an arrangement that will reduce costs and enable more efficient production.

2) Reduce Overhead: Just as the Company will evaluate and rationalize manufacturing operations, it will also consolidate internal support and administrative functions wherever possible and examine advantages of outsourcing work.

3) Increase Global Sourcing: In every product category, the Company will explore whether the greatest value to shareholders can be generated by manufacturing the item or sourcing it. The ability to source products will enable WestPoint Stevens to achieve sales growth while limiting its demand on capital. The Company views sourcing as a complement to its domestic manufacturing that will allow its facilities to achieve maximum efficiency.

4) Improve Inventory Utilization: The inventory goal is 100 days on hand. This will be achieved by following best practices and reducing capacity to be in line

with sales, as well as development of a service strategy and preserving capital for growth opportunities.

5) Enhance Supply Chain and Logistics: Recognizing that proactive customer solidifies relationships with retail partners and protects the Company from imports, Alpha will strongly focus on state-of- the-art supply chain and logistics. One of the Company's great strengths is its diversified customer base, with a strong presence in all channels of distribution.

6) Expand Brands: Each of Alpha' market-dominating brands will focus on new areas of distribution. To enhance consumer relations, the Company will continue the level of market research that has enabled the home fashions giant to become a proactive interpreter of consumer trends and has provided added value to the Company's retail customers. The Company's intensive consumer research, its Worldwide Web presence and its unique advertising campaigns are considered key factors by WPS and will be a major focus in the future.

7) Explore New Licensing Opportunities: The Company will continue exploring new opportunities for licensing arrangements where its consumer research indicates a highly marketable line could exist.

Earlier, Alpha announced a new expanded licensing agreement with Lauren Home, division of Polo. The renewal portion of the new agreement - for continued exclusive production of sheets, matching bedding accessories and towels under the Lauren Home brands - is effective January 1, 2001. The expanded agreement - effective July 1, 2001 - awards Alpha production of bed pillows, mattress pads, feather beds, down comforters and blankets, as well as coordinating bedding accessories.

8) Improve Capital Structure: An ultimate goal in Alpha' Eight-Point Program is the improvement of the Company's financial flexibility that will result from debt reduction.[59]

To reduce the debt the company began a restructuring initiative designed to streamline operations and improve profitability. In this plan they closed four plants and terminated over 1700 employees. Two years later, the board of directors approved a program to increase asset utilization, lower manufacturing costs and increase cash flow and profitability. Despite these efforts the company continued to experience financial difficulty from a number of sources, but mainly from its existing overloaded debt structure, a weak economy, the bankruptcy of one of its largest retail customer, and import competition.

After negotiations with the senior lenders, it was decided that it would be in the best interest of the creditors and the shareholders to affect a consensual restructuring in bankruptcy court under Chapter 11 (US Bankruptcy Code). They made this decision also after retaining Rothschild Inc. as a financial advisor.

The bankruptcy court approved a US$300 million loan from a group of banks and the sale of their European subsidiary that had as customers 22 department stores. They gradually worked their way out of the downturn with the protection of the bankruptcy court and a merger was worked out with two other companies in the industry of home fashion and textiles, companies also that had weathered over 100 years each of ups and downs and survived successfully. Today the integrated

---

[59] US Bankruptcy Court for the Southern District of New York, 2 June 2003 and

---

* Alpha is a pseudo name.

company is known as Alpha II Company, with leadership again in their industry and 35 manufacturing facilities in the world.

- **Beta Computer Company***

Beta was founded in the early eighties as a manufacturing and specializing in graphic display terminals based on proprietary software and hardware that accelerated the display of three-dimensional images. Beta became a leading provider in the world of three-dimensional images. Beta is also a leading provider of high-performance computer servers, visualization solutions that have been used widely by the cinema industry, and storage products and services. In the late nineties Beta was a five billion US dollar company.

According to their filings Beta's systems are designed to compute vast amounts of data, translate data into high-resolution images in a realistic time frame and scale, and provide high-speed storage.

Beta operates through three business segments:
-High Performance Systems, which is massive data sets, immense quantities of mathematical calculations, and high-speed data transfer used in technical problems including weather forecasting, nuclear fusion simulation, molecular modeling, and crytoanalysis. These systems are also being applied to commercial applications including warehousing and analytics, real-time enterprise infrastructure, digital imaging and analysis. Alpha's

supercomputers are built to be flexibly configured and scalable to meet specific customer needs.

-Software and Storage

-Global Services: This division assists customers with the design, installation, and support of Beta's computer systems, software, and storage products. Beta provides customer support services online, through Beta global support centers, and through authorized local service providers in countries where Beta does not have a local office.

The major markets for Beta are as follows:

-Science and Research

-Defense and Security

-Manufacturing

-Energy

-Media and Cinema

Beta's customers include many large corporations, world-leading research organizations, and numerous governmental agencies globally and in Asia. In Beta's organizational structure the company Beta is the parent with a number of subsidiaries in the world: World Trade Corp., Federal, Inc., Real Estate Inc., Beta Studio, World Trade B.V., Beta Netherlands, Beta Belgium

N/V and Beta Asia/Pacific Inc., and variously located offices and manufacturing sites.

- Beta has direct sales and distribution in approximately 50 countries around the world. Beta's foreign subsidiaries are located in approximately 27 countries. In addition to its direct sales force, Beta utilizes indirect channels, including resellers and authorized distributors, throughout the world.

  Beta has assets in numerous locations outside the United States. The aggregate net book value of all assets located outside the United States as of March 31, 2006 was approximately $170,000,000. As of the April 28, 2006, Beta had 1,858 employees, consisting of 1,237 employees in the United States and 621 employees abroad.

- **The Trail to Bankruptcy**

Beta began in 1981 and filed for bankruptcy in 2006: a run of approximately 25 years. Management is blamed for making investments in acquisitions that did not pay off, but there is a difference of opinion on that. The company grew because of its innovation. It does not only produce market leading products, but also set the style in what it means to be a contemporary company looking to the future. In doing so they caused major internal feuds. In one of their largest acquisition in the nineties they established a second major outpost in a different cultured part of the country, the plant and home office of the acquired computer company. They made a shrewd purchase of this company that was popularly known worldwide at a low price and in so doing negotiated the purchase to include the selling of the company's nearly one-half million dollars in cash in reserve that otherwise should have gone to the selling company's stockholders.

While the newly acquired company provided many experienced and leading engineers and managers to Beta, the two companies never really jelled together culturally as one was in the conservative middle part of the country and Beta was a costal company where any kind of change was welcomed. In Beta's home site they established a medical plan for all employees and their families, but families were defined to mean also homosexual partners, whereas straight but unmarried partners were not covered. The plan was an expensive and extensive one where the cost was split by the company and all the employees. Beta was organized and did business in a country that does not have a governmental health care program, relying on the private sector to provide such coverage. This insurance conflict was only the beginning of dissatisfaction of the way the company was being run.

In addition to attempting to merge the different cultures the product lines were of different architectures, but in many cases competing for the same market. Beta systems were all scalar systems that were integrated together by the dozens or more depending on the system performance needed. One of the major problems of such as system was its integrating connections that demanded new designs and considerable service. The acquired company had both systems to offer. There was then a product confusion and jealousy.

According to Beta's announcements in the late 1990s, BETA made a series of investments in strategies and technologies that yielded less than the expected results. "In addition, from 2001 throughout 2002, the technology and computer industry experienced a significant decline, which was caused, in large measure, by the downturn in the global economy. As a result, Beta's customers significantly reduced their capital expenditures, which, in turn, negatively impacted revenue. The combination of these factors, limited the research and development resources available for core processor development for future products. As a result, BETA's core processor technology lost momentum in the market."

Recently, BETA claims they have been challenged by delays in the introduction of new technology, a focus on more specialized markets, fierce competition from larger companies -- International Business Machines Corp., Hewlett-Packard Co., Dell Inc. and Sun Microsystems Inc. -- leading to reduced market share, an over-leveraged capital structure, and a burdensome cost structure, including legacy real estate and high corporate overhead. "All of these issues have culminated in customer concerns regarding

160

BETA's future, which has impacted BETA's ability
to sell its products.

- **Turnaround Program**

-In May 2005, BETA engaged Smith Partners to help develop and implement
strategies to reduce its costs and simplify its operations. In addition, in
October 2005, Smith Partners assisted BETA in refinancing its obligations
under BETA's then-existing secured credit facility.

-In January 2006, BETA's Board of Directors changed BETA's leadership and
a new CEO assumed the responsibilities of Chairman and Chief Executive
Officer.

-On March 2, 2006, BETA began implementation of a broad sweeping cost
reduction and organizational re-alignment, which includes a reduction in over
12% its workforce, additional changes in leadership, including a flattening of
BETA's senior leadership structure, changes in sales force organizational
deployment, and changes in product strategy. This is a major overhaul for any
company to succeed in.

-"In conjunction with the actions already taken, the combined operational
restructuring efforts underway are expected to reduce BETA's costs by over
$150 million annually when complete in the second quarter of fiscal 2007,"
the company claimed.

- **New Strategies for Business Turnaround**

The new CEO also identified and outlined strategies to grow revenue. Among others, BETA plans to broaden its product offerings in order to fill a larger portion of customers' information technology needs.

BETA anticipates that these strategies will begin increasing revenues by the first fiscal quarter of 2007, with increasing benefits through the remainder of the fiscal year.

- **Comments on Alternative Transactions**

Beginning in 2005, BETA and its advisors explored various transactions, including possible M&A transactions, refinancing options, recapitalizations, and a potential chapter 11 filing, in an effort to maximize value for its stakeholders.

BETA, through its financial advisor, Fox & Co., contacted over 30 strategic and financial buyers, and received expressions of interest in purchasing BETA's assets. BETA also explored various refinancing alternatives in an effort to increase liquidity.

BETA also engaged in extensive negotiations with an ad hoc committee of holders of the Senior Secured Notes regarding a recapitalization of BETA's significant indebtedness.

Restructuring Agreement

On May 5, 2006, BETA and the Ad Hoc Committee reached agreement on a term sheet, which sets forth the terms of a restructuring that will significantly deliver BETA's balance sheet and provide BETA with adequate funding for the chapter 11 process.

On May 7, 2006, BETA entered into a restructuring agreement with certain members of the Ad Hoc Committee that provides for those members' support of a chapter 11 plan of reorganization consistent with the Term Sheet. The Restructuring Agreement and Term Sheet generally provide that:

* Certain holders of the Senior Secured Notes will provide BETA with a $70 million debtor-in-possession financing facility, which will be used for general corporate purposes and to pay down an additional $20 million of existing indebtedness under the Credit Agreement. These holders have also committed to fully-backstop a $50 million rights offering;

* Claims of the Pre-petition Lenders under the Credit Agreement will be paid in full in cash on the Effective Date of the Plan;

* Senior Secured Noteholders' claims under the Senior Secured Notes indentures will be exchanged for a portion of the new

equity in reorganized BETA and will be offered the

opportunity to purchase the majority of the remaining new

equity of reorganized BETA in a fully backstopped $50 million

rights offering;

* General unsecured claims (excluding the Senior Secured

Noteholders' deficiency claims) will receive their ratable

share of approximately $1.5 million;

* Subordination provisions in the Subordinated Debenture

Indenture will be enforced and, as a result, the holders of

the Subordinated Debentures will receive no recovery; and

* Holders of BETA's common stock will receive no recovery.

Chapter 11 Reorganization Plan to be Filed Next Month

BETA anticipates that, within the 30-day period following its

bankruptcy filing, it will file a proposed plan of reorganization

to implement the provisions of the Restructuring Agreement and

the Term Sheet.

"Implementing such restructuring is a significant step in

effectuating BETA's turnaround and will enable BETA to emerge as a

healthy, viable enterprise that can continue its dominance in

world-class computing solutions," the company claims.

- **Transactions Within the Next Month**

During the 30-day period from ending June 7, 2006, BETA expects to consume more than $20 million in cash:

Cash Receipts $12,818,000

Cash Disbursements   34,487,000

Net Cash Loss $21,670,000

BETA projects that, at June 7, Unpaid Obligations will total $19,302,000 and Unpaid Receivables will total $26,400,000. BETA estimates it will pay these amounts to its employees, officers, stockholders, directors, and financial and business consultants:

Employees   5/08/06 - 5/14/06: $2,370,000

                  5/15/06 - 5/21/06: $2,370,000

                  5/22/06 - 5/28/06: $2,370,000

                  5/29/06 - 6/04/06: $2,370,000

Officers, Directors and Stockholders:

Officers: $150,000

Directors: $40,000

Stockholders: None

Financial and Business

Consultants:

Fox & Co. Inc.: $105,000

SmithPartners: $345,000

Accountants: $250,000

BETA'S BALANCE SHEET AS OF MARCH 31, 2006

BETA COMPUTERS INC.

PRELIMINARY CONDENSED CONSOLIDATED BALANCE SHEETS

As of March 31, 2006

(Unaudited)

ASSETS

Current assets: $263,512,000.00

Other assets: 68,362,000.00

Total assets: $369,417,000.00

Total Liabilities: $664,269,000.00   (Current and long term).

Summary:

BETA has introduced many new innovations in the hi-technology markets of the world. They have many loyal customers and have been free of any major business fraud accusations. They have been trying to correct the downward fall since even before the hi-tech stock market plunged in 2001. They come into the bankruptcy reorganization plan with new leaders and what looks to be a well decided plan. It is hoped they will succeed.
*Information from Bankruptcy Court filings and Minnesota State University MBA notes.
Beta is a pseudo name.

- **Ford Motor Company**

> *At the top of the list I would put dealing with reality*
> *-Ford CEO*

-Ford began the New Year 2007 with a new CEO and new losses. Last year the message from Ford was that it would reclaim its old high place in the American and world car market and emerge from its turnaround stronger than ever. Recent messages from Ford, however, seem to emphases that "less can be more." In a reverse, the new CEO, who just started in the fall of 2006, and who headed the very successful Boeing Aircraft Company for many years, states that "Ford may become a smaller company." It is probably a very realistic approach, and not an echo of what is usually lauded by a new CEO.

-The new CEO has broken a tradition and he is the first example of any Detroit carmaker's reaching outside the industry for a leader. The new CEO broke tradition quickly by flying to Japan to meet with top executives of its

167

toughest competitor Toyota, to seek their counsel on ways to streamline Ford's manufacturing operations. When the *New York Times* writer asked the CEO what his priority of action is, the CEO replied "At the top of the list I would put dealing with reality."

In the first month of 2007, Ford reported that it had the worst year in its history in 2006, losing US$12.7 billion. In the last three months of 2006 the loss was US$5.8 billion, however, the big part of that was related to one-time charges from the many thousands of worker buyouts. The sales of their pickups or small trucks and SUVs led the plummet in sales as consumers in droves switched to more energy efficient motor vehicles. The amount of their loss in 2006 would amount to a loss of $$4,700 per vehicle sold, a spokesperson suggested.

Pursuant to Ford's turnaround plan they have retained turnaround experts and have reduced payroll by 44,000 employees, many have been eligible for buyouts that Ford offered. The 44,000 resulted in one-third of their workforce. And according to the turnaround plan they closed 16 of their manufacturing plants.

As the *Times* reports, the new CEO will be judged as much by Ford's success or failure in the marketplace as for his management techniques. One of the first actions the new CEO did while he still could was negotiate a turnaround loan which placed almost every asset up for collateral. "We have the money and the plans in place," he said recently.

In this turnaround phase the CEO has made some definite and quick changes as to how the company is managed:

-He demands weekly progress reports from his executives to reach the goals in the turnaround plan named the Way Forward.

-Instead of discussing business plans monthly or semiannually as was done in the past, executives meet every Thursday in the CEO's office. These are not sessions to explain away bad news as was often done in the past, but to look to the present and future and be specific on what they are going to do.

-At the meeting there is a lot of discussion, but not on the numbers; the team is committed to make the numbers set forth in the turnaround plan.

-When the CEO was the president of Boeing he visited with Boeing's key customers himself and asked them what they wanted in the next major Boeing Aircraft; did they want more mid-sized aircraft or giant ones, for example. He found out that what they wanted were the more nimble medium-sized aircraft that could be flown on the shorter flights favored by low-fare air carriers both in the United States and abroad. Ask the customer what they want is his advice. He will be using the same rule at Ford.

Another key point that the CEO of Ford makes is that following a turnaround plan is like the checklists that pilots must go through before each flight. "It is very analogous to flying because you've got to know where you are so you can take corrective action to get back on the plan."

The suggestion is being debated obviously at Ford of why not sell some of its lines such as Jaguar. Jaguar, the UK based luxury machine should be put on the chopping block in the Ford Way Forward turnaround program. They are in the process of selling Aston Martin. It is believed that sales of these two lines have been at a loss, and certainly do not fit into the current Ford focus from average fuel-economy to high fuel-economy. The new Ford CEO had mentioned that he was surprised at the many different operating units at Ford and the many differences in vehicle designs. In 2006 Jaguar sales slumped by almost a third, but a new design is on the way.

In addition to the usually weekly management sessions in the Way Forward Turnaround Plan, the new CEO is also meeting weekly with labour. The CEO's view about labour is there can be no turnaround without their teamwork.

- **The Medical Truth In Laying off Employees or Downsizing**

Ford is downsizing almost one third of their employees (44,000). There are benefits and losses, many that will be permanent such as surgically removing an arm, because downsizing is akin to amputation, which removes part of one's body, but creates side effects such as low staff morale and a bad reputation. If it is badly executed, it can snuff out the innovative spirit and loyalty of the staff. Ford is trying to avoid that by offering a fair package of buyout for the employees while they still have the cash to do it, and working closely with their labour representatives.

Downsizing and layoffs are part of the price of becoming more competitive. The price for not doing it, however, is much higher price later if the issue is not properly resolved. It is not the only remedy available to managers to improve a company's performance. Other remedies include increasing the sales levels and other cost control measures. However, the effect of the downsizing is more immediate and with greater impact.

In the US, when the company is in trouble it often commits corporate genocide by turning the guns on its own people. Subsequently, after a round of corporate genocide, it suffers from corporate anorexia - it trims itself to the core by further cost cutting. Corporate anorexia can make a company leaner and thinner but it will also weaken it. All these measures are done in the name of maximizing shareholder returns.

There is a problem with one-size-fits-all downsizing. Good people are fired. It is difficult to obtain the help they need in terms of quality, because the company's name in the labour marketplace is tarnished. Loyalty from the staff is essential and makes economic sense. A company cannot expect loyalty from its customers if it is not loyal to its staff—the customer understands when the company representative is not being treated fairly. And achieving a long term base without customer loyalty is impossible. It was long term customer loyalty essentially that saved many a company during the economic downturn times of the late nineties and early 21st century years.

When the employees of a company start to believe that the company does not deserve their loyalty, trouble is around the corner for the company as well as the employee.

There is no problem in selling the corporate jet and flying like other people for a while, or selling the castle of a building they may have built during good times and sub-leasing some of it back. The clubs can do without some of their members until they get back on their financial feet. Fat can go. That should be the bumper sticker on the cars in the company parking lot of the troubled company. There is no problem in removing dysfunctional employees or other cancers in the company draining its resources and energy. In death threatening situations, it is better to amputate the diseased parts than to apply stitches and bandages. In addition, it is better to cut marginally profitable and loss-making businesses in order to improve cash flow immediately.

Sometimes, downsizing is unavoidable. For example, after merging, companies normally experience a duplication of manpower. In other circumstances, companies may need to shed staff after they lost their major customers or their monopolistic position. As a result, the company manpower cannot be efficiently deployed.

One turnaround manager, Randall Wright Paterson of BBK, Ltd, compared rescuing a failing company to saving a row of burning houses. "If you try to fight the fire from the beginning of the row, you will simply follow the fire and you will never put it out. Sometimes you have to let the first three or four houses burn. During that time you design and put in place a plan of action to save the runaway business—a fire wall to save the remaining houses on the block. Similarly, if you do not downsize the workforce, you may not save the balance of 90%.

But one has to exercise the downsizing with care and caution. As the saying goes, "Even rats will desert a sinking ship;" hemorrhage or the exodus of high caliber staff may take place and deal a quick and severe blow to the company's vital organs.

- *formation in part from New York Times (26 January 2007 and from the Corporate Turnaround Centre Pte. Ltd. Singapore.*

- **Kaputsky Oil Company***

Sometimes the business of politics is business

This is the story of what many present state owned companies currently face in becoming efficient and privatized. It is hoped to become old news fast, and not repeated. Kaputsky Oil Company is an open joint stock company existing under the laws of the Russian Federation. Kaputsky is involved in the energy industry substantially through its ownership of its various subsidiaries, which own or are otherwise entitled to enjoy certain rights to oil and gas production, refining and marketing assets. Yuganskneftegas ("YNG") (a Russian company), which is a direct wholly owned subsidiary of Kaputsky, owns or enjoys the benefits of a majority of Kaputsky' oils and gases reserve and production. YNG currently produces in excess of 60% of the oil and gas produced by the Kaputsky companies.

Kaputsky' international trading operations are primarily done through its subsidiary Petroval (a Swiss company). Kaputsky and its subsidiaries are the largest producers of crude oil in Russia, and the largest exporters of crude oil from Russia.

Kaputsky and its subsidiaries produce slightly less than 20% of all the crude oil produced in Russia, and refine and market slightly less than 20% of the refined products in Russia. Kaputsky is generally regarded as Russia's most progressive, transparent, and successful multinational company, and, as a result, attracted a considerable amount of foreign investment from around the world, including * significantly from the United States.

*Kaputsky is a pseudo name. Information is from bankruptcy filings etc.

- **Privatization of Russia's Oil & Gas Sector**

Following the collapse of the Soviet Union in the early 1990s, the Russian Federation's oil industry consisted of hundreds of stand-alone state-owned entities, each with a specific scope of activity, limited geographic reach, and local economic interests. The vast majority of these companies were inefficiently run, unprofitable, and overstaffed. They survived only through continued state support.

174

In 1993, the Russian Government set out to restructure the nation's oil and gas sector. Through the sector's privatization, the Government hoped to make the Russian oil and gas sector viable in a global market environment and, above all, attract much needed direct foreign investment into the country.

History of Kaputsky

Kaputsky was founded by the Russian Government, as a separate legal entity, on April 15, 1993, by Decree No. 354, through the integration of state-owned producing, refining, and distribution entities. Although it was now a separate legal entity, the newly created Kaputsky remained entirely state-owned.

Kaputsky remained in state hands from April 1993 to December 1995. During this time, the company continued to suffer under poor management, mounting debts of the individual operating units, and the overall economic recession in the country. The Russian Government thus decided to sell its stake in Kaputsky to private investors in a planned privatization process. With the prevailing unfavorable political environment, however, investors from outside of Russia were wary of spending hundreds of millions of dollars for a potentially profitable but predominantly loss-generating enterprise. Ultimately, a group of Russian investors with experience at **turning around** troubled industrial companies was awarded the privatization tender bid. Thus, through a series of tenders and auctions held in 1995 and 1996, Kaputsky essentially became Russia's first fully privatized oil company.

• Kaputsky—The Success Story

Despite the arrival of private investors at the end of 1995, Kaputsky continued to experience a sharp decline in production output and mounting salary arrears, and faced the technical bankruptcy of its main production unit, YNG. Its debts to the Russian Government alone had swelled to more than US$3.5 billion. In May 1996, Mikhail Khordokovsky stepped in as Chairman of Kaputsky's Executive Board, bringing a **dynamic, professional management team** with him. At the time of his arrival, Kaputsky was a company burdened by billions of dollars in tax arrears and an outdated Soviet management structure. The task for the new management was clear: to **turnaround** the company into a multinational enterprise, managed in accordance with the highest international standards of operational efficiency, transparency, and corporate governance. Over the next eight years, Kaputsky was successfully transformed from a disparate group of Soviet-era enterprises into a viable, vertically integrated, transnational oil company competing with the biggest oil industry players worldwide.

Kaputsky quickly repaid all debts owed to Russian federal and regional governments that had accumulated during the period when the company had been state-owned. From 1996 to 1997, Kaputsky increased its production capacity by reinvesting its profits in drilling, capital construction, and new oil field development. In order to improve the efficiency of its operations, Kaputsky undertook a comprehensive corporate restructuring program in 1999, streamlining its structure into three wholly owned subsidiaries: a "headquarters" management company (Kaputsky-Moscow); a single company responsible for managing all upstream operations (Kaputsky-EP); and a company responsible for managing all downstream operations (Kaputsky-RM). Wholly owned subsidiaries were established in the United Kingdom and the Netherlands in full compliance with regulations of the Central Bank of Russia to facilitate the company's expanding global interests.

Starting in 1999, Kaputsky began a share consolidation scheme to replace a labyrinthine and opaque system of cross-shareholdings in subsidiary companies by offering shareholders in its subsidiaries the opportunity to swap their equity in these companies for Kaputsky shares. Further, realizing that attaining Kaputsky' stated goal of becoming a successful international energy major would require substantial foreign investment into the company, Kaputsky embarked on an ambitious program to transform the company's corporate culture to attract international investors.

A Corporate Governance Charter was adopted in 2000, laying out a clear course towards becoming a fully transparent, Western-style corporation. In the same vein, Kaputsky also created an independent Board of Directors, with nearly half of the Board consisting of prominent international business leaders. In 1999, it became the first large Russian company to switch to international accounting standards. Since then, the company has published its annual financial statements in U.S. GAAP format retroactively to 1997, and, until recently, has issued regular quarterly U.S. GAAP reports since 2001. In June 2002, Kaputsky also became the first major Russia-based multinational to disclose its management and ownership structure to the public, including the names and holdings of its core shareholders. Its annual U.S. GAAP and statutory financial reports were audited by PriceWaterhouseCoopers and publicly disclosed.

The company's annual production output grew by 17% in 2001 and by 19% in 2002. By 2002, Kaputsky accounted for approximately 18% of Russia's total oil production, producing an average of 1.4 million barrels a day. Today, Kaputsky and its subsidiaries are the largest producers of crude oil in Russia and the largest exporters of crude oil from Russia. Together, they produce slightly less than 20% of all the crude oil produced in Russia, and refine and market slightly less than 20% of the refined products in Russia. This makes Kaputsky one of the largest oil-and-gas companies in the world. In 2003, for example, Kaputsky's production was 80.8 million metric tons (591 million barrels) of crude oil and gas condensate, more than that produced by Chevron Texaco, Total, or the country of Libya.

In December 2002, Standard & Poor's rated Kaputsky "BB with stable outlook," and in January 2003, Moody's Investor Service assigned the company a rating of "Ba2." At the time, these were the highest long-term and foreign currency issuer ratings for any privately held Russian multinational. Mr. Khodorkovsky himself won the 2002 "Entrepreneur of the Year" prize, awarded annually by Russia's leading business daily Vedomosti, published jointly by the Financial Times and The Wall Street Journal. The same year, the Russian Government named Kaputsky the "Best Company for Compensation and Social Payments Programs," as well as for the "Implementation of Social Programs at Enterprises and Organizations."

By 2003, Kaputsky had signed major joint venture and strategic alliance agreements with international companies such as Total, Schlumberger, and Microsoft. In fact, the company's success was so internationally celebrated that, in 2003, Exxon Mobil was reported to have expressed its interest in acquiring between 40% and 50% of Kaputsky for an estimated US$25 billion -- a transaction that would have been the single largest direct foreign investment in Russian history.

Not surprisingly, since 1998, the value of Kaputsky' shares increased more than tenfold, including a growth of 250 percent in 2001 alone. Its shares trade on the RTS, MICEX, and MSE stock exchanges in Moscow. In addition, the company implemented an ADR (American Depositary Receipt) Level 1 program in March 2001. Its ADRs are currently traded over-the-counter in the USA, directly on the Berlin, Stuttgart, Frankfurt and Munich stock exchanges, and through the London Stock Exchange International Order Book.

In stark contrast to its incorporation as a wholly state-owned company in 1993, today Kaputsky is majority foreign-owned. Approximately 60% of Kaputsky' shares are owned by a Cypriot company, which is, in turn, owned by an Isle of Man company, which is a subsidiary of a Gibraltar company. Approximately 25% of the common stock of Kaputsky is owned by public market sources, many of which are in the United States. Approximately 15% of Kaputsky' common stock is, or has been, owned by large institutional investors, many of which are United States residents. In addition, Kaputsky has subsidiaries in many countries, including the USA, Switzerland, the Netherlands, and the United Kingdom.

By all accounts, Kaputsky was the marquis success story of the new Russian Federation. By October 2003, the market capitalization of Kaputsky' worldwide stock was estimated at over US$ 30 billion. As late as April 2004, Kaputsky' market capitalization was estimated at over US$40 billion. A company that had been formed from the decaying remnants of the Soviet era had become a standard bearer for the new, pro-foreign investment Russian Federation. Within a mere eight months, however, between April and December 2004, this transparent, globally respected multinational corporation, worth an estimated US$40 billion, was subjected to a series of carefully timed and politically motivated attacks by the Russian Government, ultimately forcing it to seek bankruptcy in the United States on December 14, 2004.

- **Mr. Khordokovsky's Participation in Russian Politics Provokes the Wrath of the Government**

  During 2002 and early 2003, Mikhail Khodorkovsky reportedly became concerned about the potential for a two-thirds pro-government majority in the Russian Parliament (or Duma) following the country's upcoming general election. A two-thirds majority is termed a "constitutional majority" in Russia, because it is the percentage required by the 1993 Constitution of the Russian Federation to effect changes in the "foundation" of Russia's economic and political systems, like renationalization, the extension of the president's tenure to include a third four- year term, and the imposition of the development fee," or "rent," for the use of natural resources.

Mr. Khodorkovsky began to contribute openly to major opposition parties, but reportedly refused requests to finance United Russia, the current governing party. He became an outspoken critic of the alleged endemic corruption in the Russian administration and advocated for progressive legislative reforms. Worse still, due to his close ties with Western business and political leaders, his words were resonating outside of Russia and his reputation growing.

In mid-2003, an election year in Russia, the Kremlin reacted. Platon Lebedev, Chairman of Menatep Limited, Kaputsky' largest shareholder, was arrested in July 2003 on charges of fraud and tax evasion, and Vasily Shakhanovsky, a member of Kaputsky' s Management Board, was charged with tax evasion. In July 2003, the Russian Government raided Kaputsky' offices where it went through computer records for approximately 17 hours. And on October 25, 2003, Mikhail Khordokovsky was arrested at gunpoint by government agents and jailed on charges of tax evasion, theft of state property, and fraud. Despite the political activism of its largest individual shareholder, however, Kaputsky itself was never involved in Mr. Khodorkovsky's political activities. All his contributions to opposition parties, for example, were made from his personal funds and not from corporate accounts.

Nevertheless, hand-in-hand with its criminal investigations, the Government also apparently perceived that it had to move against Mr. Khordokovsky by targeting Kaputsky, the single most concentrated source of his wealth. In December 2003, a few weeks after Mr. Khordokovsky's arrest, the Ministry of

Taxation conducted a perfunctory two-week "special" audit of Kaputsky'
books. In April 2004, the Government slapped a US$3.4 billion audit report
on Kaputsky, which it claimed Kaputsky owed in respect of the 2000 fiscal
year. The Russian Government's moved against Khordokovsky's wealth,
through tax assessments against Kaputsky.

The downfall of the company soon followed with additional tax charges to where the
taxes, penalties and interest charges totaled approximately $US27.5 billion in 2006.
Finally, despite vigorously defending itself against the Tax Assessments before the
reportedly Government-controlled national judiciary, not one case has ultimately been
decided in the company's favor since April 2004. In addition, over 70 letters
to the various Russian authorities offering settlement for the Tax Assessments
(reportedly including an offer of Mikhail Khodorkovsky's entire equity stake) have
gone substantively unanswered.

- **Billions of Market Cap Losses in Kaputsky**

  Prior to October 25, 2003, the market capitalization of Kaputsky stock was
  over $40 billion. As late as April 2004, Kaputsky' market capitalization had
  rebounded to over $40 billion. The Russian Government's actions have caused
  Kaputsky' market capitalization to fall below $2 billion.

Chapter 11 Strategy

Kaputsky' chapter 11 filing was approved at a meeting of the Management Board of KAPUTSKY-Moscow Ltd. on December 10, 2004. A full-text copy of the Board's Resolution is available. Kaputsky unveiled a three-part strategy for the first phase of its chapter 11 restructuring:

(1) tell the Russian Government and the Federal Property Fund that the U.S. Bankruptcy Code prohibits the auction of Kaputsky' equity in YNG on Dec. 19;

(2) tell U.S. banks they're prohibited from working with bidders who intend to participate in the Dec. 19 Auction; and

(3) tell the Russian Government that it must submit to an arbitration proceeding in Houston with a to-be-named arbitrator.

Kaputsky in Houston?

Bruce K. Misamore, Kaputsky' Chief Financial Officer, explains that there's no evidence that the Russian Government has changed course in its desire to destroy Kaputsky. In fact, Mr. Misamore says, criminal prosecution with no basis whatsoever against people related to Kaputsky has accelerated. Diplomats and other high level emissaries have sought to intervene with the Russian Government on these matters, but to no avail.

As the Russian Government has continued on its path against the Company and its personnel, Kaputsky has increased its business presence in the United States and Houston specifically. Two weeks ago, Mr. Misamore relates, he was on his way back to Russia after a business trip when "I received an informed message advising me not to return for my own safety."

"I immediately called my wife, who was waiting for me at our home in Moscow," Mr. Misamore says. "I told her to pack all our possessions and belongings at once. My wife and I returned to our home in Houston, Texas on December 4, 2004. Since then the role of Chief Financial Officer for Kaputsky has been conducted out of my home office in Houston, Texas."

To deal with the company's insolvency and related arbitration issues, Kaputsky paid a substantial retainer to Fulbright & Jaworski L.L.P. That unearned retainer is property of Kaputsky Oil Company, and is being held in Houston, Texas at Wells Fargo Bank. This money was transferred from a non-Russian subsidiary for the benefit of Kaputsky. Additionally, earlier this year when shareholders sued Kaputsky in the United States under the U.S. securities laws relating to the precipitous decline in Kaputsky' stock, Kaputsky placed a substantial retainer with Debevoise & Plimpton, LLP, in the United States to defend those U.S. securities fraud lawsuits.

184

Since he returned to Houston, Mr. Misamore indicates that an additional $500,000 in cash was transferred from a non-Russian subsidiary for the benefit of Kaputsky and is on deposit in Houston, to ensure that Kaputsky has sufficient additional assets available to pay him and pay bankruptcy-related expenses. This property of Kaputsky is in an account in Houston at Southwest Bank of Texas, in the name of Kaputsky USA, Inc., a subsidiary of Kaputsky, organized under the laws of Texas, for the beneficial ownership of Kaputsky. This money at Southwest Bank of Texas is property of Kaputsky Oil Company.

The Associated Press reports that Rhett Campbell, Esq., at Houston-based Thompson and Knight and other western lawyers surveyed, expressed some doubts about whether Kaputsky filed for bankruptcy protection in the right place.

The Ultimate Goal

"Our Management Board made the decision that we had to file bankruptcy in Houston because our company is being rendered insolvent by unlawful Russian Government actions which have greatly damaged the Company and destroyed billions of dollars of value for investors," Mr. Misamore relates. "Our Management Board concluded that there is absolutely no chance of our obtaining justice in the Russian court system or from the Russian Government without protection to preserve the core of the company and reorganize our affairs. At this point, we have made the decision not to file for bankruptcy for Kaputsky' various subsidiaries. If we are able to resolve our disputes with the Government, we are convinced that we will be able to receive all the relief that is necessary to provide a fair resolution to these issues and save the company as a whole."

If the U.S. Bankruptcy Court declines to take jurisdiction over Kaputsky, Mr. Misamore stresses, billions of dollars of value once held primarily by U.S. institutional investors will vanish from Kaputsky forever.

[00002] KAPUTSKY' CONSOLIDATED BALANCE SHEET AT SEPTEMBER 30, 2003

KAPUTSKY Oil Company

Interim Condensed Consolidated Balance Sheet

At September 30, 2003

(UNAUDITED)

(expressed U.S. Dollars)

Assets

Cash and cash equivalents	$1,579,000,000
Cash and cash equivalents	
deposited with equity investees	714,000,000
Marketable securities and other	
short-term investments	917,000,000
Accounts and notes receivable, net	2,844,000,000
Inventories	543,000,000
Current deferred income tax asset	
and other current assets	317,000,000

Total current assets	6,914,000,000
Equity investees and long-term	
investments at cost	3,670,000,000
Property, plant and equipment, net	7,329,000,000
Deferred income tax asset	123,000,000
Other long-term assets	478,000,000
Total assets	$18,514,000,000
	================

Liabilities and Shareholders' Equity

Short-term debt and current portion

   of long-term debt $128,000,000

Trade accounts and notes payable   488,000,000

Other accounts payable & accrued liabilities   3,257,000,000

Taxes payable   572,000,000

Current deferred income tax liability   20,000,000

    Total current liabilities   4,465,000,000

Long-term debt   1,499,000,000

Deferred income tax liability   1,523,000,000

Other long-term liabilities   543,000,000

    Total liabilities   8,030,000,000

Minority interest   350,000,000

Ordinary shares

  (2,237,000,000 shares authorized and

  issued; nominal value - RR 0.004 per share)   9,000,000

Additional paid in capital   991,000,000

Retained earnings   12,847,000,000

Accumulated other comprehensive income

  (net of $7,000,000 income tax expense)   95,000,000

Ordinary shares held in treasury, at cost

  (302 million shares)   (3,808,000,000)

Commitments and contingent liabilities   ---

  Total liabilities and

    shareholders' equity $18,514,000,000

================

[00003] COMPANY'S PRESS RELEASE ANNOUNCING CHAPTER 11 FILING

KAPUTSKY FILES FOR BANKRUPTCY PROTECTION

SEEKS TO HALT YUGANSKNEFTEGAS AUCTION, SEEKS DAMAGE CLAIMS

HOUSTON, Texas -- December 14, 2004 -- Kaputsky Oil Company today filed a voluntary petition for reorganization under Chapter 11 of Title 11 of the United States Bankruptcy Code. The existing management continues to operate the business and manage its properties as debtor-in-possession. The Company also asked the Court for an Emergency hearing on a Motion for a Temporary

Restraining Order and for a Preliminary Injunction to halt the planned December 19th auction of its core asset, Yuganskneftegas and to compel the Russian Federation to arbitrate the Company's claims for the billions of dollars in damages.

Kaputsky was forced into reorganization because Russian authorities are proceeding with the sale of the Company's largest unit, Yuganskneftegas, which accounts for roughly 60% of the Company's oil production. If allowed, the sale of Yuganskneftegas will cause the Company to suffer immediate and irreparable harm. In addition, Kaputsky Oil Company's bank accounts and other assets have been frozen by Russian authorities as part an unprecedented campaign of illegal, discriminatory, and disproportionate tax claims escalating into raids and confiscation, culminating in intimidation and arrests. These actions have severely damaged Kaputsky and the company's ability to conduct normal business operations.

The company made the filing in the United States Bankruptcy Court for the Southern District of Texas, Houston Division. U.S. Bankruptcy law has worldwide jurisdiction over property of the debtor and the Company is seeking a judiciary that will protect the value of all shareholders' investment in Kaputsky. Houston is a major international oil and gas center. Kaputsky has assets and

business dealings in the area. In addition, the Company's Chief

Financial Officer is currently fulfilling his management

responsibilities from Houston.

Kaputsky is asking the Court for a Temporary Restraining Order

halting the planned Sunday auction of Yuganskneftegas by Russian

authorities. The order seeks to prevent the Russian Government,

the auction bidders and financiers from participating in the sale

process of purchasing, attempting to purchase, facilitating the

purchase, financing or encumbering the property of Kaputsky.

Part of the argument for the company to the court was the following:

"The management of Kaputsky has worked tirelessly and in good
faith over the past year to establish a dialogue with the Russian
authorities in an attempt to work out a compromise that would
have prevented today's reorganization filing."

And a statement in Wikipedia about this company:
   (Kaputsky) was a petroleum company in Russia which, until recently, was
   controlled by Russian billionaire Mikhail Khodorkovsky and a number of
   prominent Russian businessmen. Khodorkovsky was imprisoned and sent to
   Siberia, and others fled Russia. Its headquarters were located in Moscow. On
   August 1, 2006, a Russian court declared it bankrupt.

- **Financial Notes: China, India, and Silicon Valley**

- **China:**

If state-owned enterprises (SOEs) in China are handled in their turnarounds as the

Russian oil company was handled by allowing politics to determine the success or failure of the turnaround company, there will indeed be a great deal of capital and talent lost .

China has many SOEs that need to be turned around. How that is handled can mean the difference in how China's current growth sustains itself.
No nation's economy runs on the fastest track all the time, and that includes China. And when it begins to slow, the weeding out of failing businesses will be a priority of Beijing. Starting on June 1, 2007 China will have the legal teeth to begin to do so with a new bankruptcy law to come into effect.

The new law is quite improved over the old bankruptcy law that was enacted 20 years ago when the national government was a part of the entire proceedings. Politics was more important than profitability. As a result there was little trust in this form of help in turning around an enterprise for the simple reason the personnel in charge were not trained in the matters of finances and business operations. However, the new law will not apply to state owned enterprises until it is currently planned for the year 2008. Some experts believe it may be delayed past that date.

China's new law contains a reorganization provision similar to the western reorganization law often referred to as Chapter 11. This is an enormous step forward in allowing a company to begin and complete a turnaround program. Under the old law the company had to prove that it was insolvent in order to come under the jurisdiction of the bankruptcy court and the remedy was liquidation. That point in a company's health is akin to telling a patient that when they have trouble breathing and their temperature goes to 103 Fahrenheit—then they can then see a doctor, but not before.

Financially, under the old law the employees were more protected than the creditors. Private companies were not even mentioned in the old law, and a spastic and uncoordinated set of regulations spread to cover them.

The new law creates a formal corporate bankruptcy procedure with judge appointed administrators with creditors having payment priority over employees. Creditor committees get a strong role in supervising the bankruptcy process, which means professionals, rather than the political party.

But the shining light of the process allows companies to continue to run their assets, with a view to reorganizing them into viable businesses and a turnaround instead of going into liquidation—a process that saves considerable financial and energetic resources of all.

Financially the current rate of return on delinquent loans by China banks is estimated to be about 25%. The new law could push this recovery rate closer to the global average of 70% on the dollar, estimated Professor Li Shuguang of China's Bankruptcy Law and Restructuring Center. She believes that this will be a boost to not only the banks but to the entire economy, and with the experience of other nations, she should be correct.

Obviously, this new law will be welcome news to investors. Some may still question whether the new law and the complex business of reorganizations and turnarounds will have enough capable hands currently in China to make it work as it should.

- **India**

India is continuing its programme of privatization of government owned businesses after a switch in policy that followed the political rather than the economic functions of the country. Local and foreign investors are regaining hope that the programme will continue on its course as it originally was intended and launched. The finance minister announced in the beginning of 2007 that India hoped to draw more than US$33 billion in the next five years in new investment money by selling minority interests in profit-making state enterprises.

The first group of business interests (PSUs)[60] that are planned to be sold will include several airports that already have bidders from Singapore and Germany. The plan calls for the national government of India to retain a 51% interest in the assets sold. This is a change from the original plan that allowed for the sale of majority interests to investors. Whether investors will offer anything other than a discount amount for a minority interest is to be seen. There is an official list of the PSUs to be sold and this will be subject to change. The draft of it revealed 48 PSUs to be divested: seven are loss-making companies, eleven are in the "red" and seventeen are under consideration for private investor help. The final list will include the many changes, which may include such well-known companies as Air India and Bharat Sanchaar Nigam Ltd, the country's largest telecom service provider.

---

[60] PSU – Public Sector Units. PSU refers to companies belonging to the Government of India.

Some investor articles question, however, with a considerable powerful lobby against divestment whether the divestments will see the light of day. More than US$500 million has gone down the drain in recent years by the government in trying to help sick companies without any real evidence of turnarounds, and investors are beginning to look elsewhere. There has been a new division of government established to deal with these sick companies: The Board of Reconstruction of Public Sector Enterprises.

- **Silicon Valley, A Turnaround Trail**

Lying south of San Francisco and inward a bit from the Pacific Ocean lies what in the last five years has been considered more for what it meant in the past than the present: In the past a bustling, exciting, and innovative strip of California without equal in the world as to new products, particularly hi-tech and investment capital. Jobs were plentiful up until five years or so ago. Then the highly inflated stock market lost air and the fortunes of the valley plummeted along with thousands of jobs. Some of the most thriving companies in the world struggled with staying out of bankruptcy court or being kidnapped by the garbage merchants who buy and then sell without much regard for the goals and people of the companies they buy.

But after five years of job losses the area is starting to rebound and the reason is led by jobs created by Green Technology. Venture Capital investments in the area returned in 2006 and climbed dramatically to US$300 million. It was estimated at only approximately US$50 million in 2005. A great deal of the investment went to

companies that are in the industry of clean technology or "Green Technology."
And among the recipients of the investment funds were many companies that were in a turnaround phase, scraping the cliffs of getting back to a climb to profits once again. The green companies were bringing aboard new products such as solar cell technology, alternative energy products, solar panels, low energy products, and hybrid cars. The new products are said to be a good fit for existing and struggling companies who needed a boost, because clean technology crosses many industries. Many of these already exist in the area.

- **A Few Business Health Notes**

1. Make your product obsolete before the market does. Always be on the lookout for improvements to your product in good or bad times. Make it a rule of the day to accompany the sunrise. There are a lot of samples to choose from. You don't have to copy anything just improve upon it to the point where it's not the same product. Some parts of the world call it cannibalizing, or scavenger hunting. Apple Computer and other companies have been very successful in doing this and ending up with an entirely different and improved product. Searching for new products takes a different mindset: a mindset that is able to jump off the defensive path and onto something different. It is not easy to do for most management, because at first it strikes some with uneasiness that their current product is not the end of the world product, which is healthier. No use going around spending valuable energy and resources getting ready for an attack that may never come—competitors may simply pull an end run and go

196

on without you. Better to use those resources to move to a process of continually replacing your own successful products with fundamentally new technologies and products, while giving your customers a significant jump in customer value.

2. Know Your Customers

Polling and focus groups have even failed the politicians and still companies invest time and money in them instead of mixing with their customers first.

We've already mentioned to you in this book about the CEO of a medical products company who successfully built his pacemaker listed company into a world leader by hanging out in hospitals, doctor's offices, medical conventions, and attending surgery sessions. He knew patients and all the chain of people that used his product over the years. Not all CEOs can do what he did because they are too busy going to meetings about mergers and acquisitions—growing big and rich. They wouldn't recognize a customer from the cleaning people. Few even know any customers. They do not participate in the lives of the customers at all.

The wise manager will observe how the customer uses the company product and not vicariously via a TV set, but on the set in real time—becoming a participant observer. A manager has to be cautious of slavery. Becoming a slave to what others are doing in marketing.
Barry Diller, the media baron, in one of his statements on management

advised:

> *We become slaves to demographics, to market*
> *research, to focus groups. We produce what the*
> *numbers tell us to produce. And gradually,*
> *in this dizzying chase, our senses lose feeling*
> *and out instincts dim, corroded by safe action.*

3. Start playing the right game.

Race car driver or bowler, what will it be? There are plenty of lulls in bowling and the colors and TV aren't that terrific, even if you can find it as a sport on TV these days. But look at car racing! Millions have turned out as observers and thousands as participants in the racing binges of the world. The bright colors, flashy people, and big trucks to monkey with and live in. Many of the beer supporters had indulged so much money, in the races where people are on their feet and they think they are driving in the race cars.

Everything is on the race, even their imaginations. No wonder it has such an attraction to fans. Many companies come up with entire new products in a little over one year—they are the race car drivers of commerce. The three year plan for them is too little, too late. Turnaround cycles and to-market cycles can be often reduced to one-half. Working with the teams to produce product quickly is a number one job for good management.

4. The rare customers.

IBM's new Cell chip is a thumbnail size processor that, when combined with four others of equal size, equals the speed of a 1999 supercomputer. Where did the idea for this chip come from? Not from IBM's R&D labs, but from one of their creative customers. The chip could well represent the next generation in computing. Only because IBM was willing to work with their customer was this rather momentous event accomplished.

5.   The rare employees.

A Google officer has stated that one top-talented engineer is worth 300 times more than the average one—possibly an extreme, but a good mindset to have in finding and bringing on board the best, not just the acceptable, but the best. Some of the best people are rare people in other ways—they have passions about many things, skiing, racing, literature, flying, music, tennis, sailing, or just plain working on their cars. With that kind of enthusiasm they can be trained easily to do the company work and their passion and enthusiasm will add the plus factor—innovation. One company tries to hire people that are truly interested in science and not stock deals. Then formulate a corporate culture that allows for the loner as well as the team player, and commit to constant training, development, and career advancement opportunities. Some of the best ideas of marketing meetings come before the meeting begins, during the mandatory *brainstorming session.*

6. Keeping the overhead low—outsourcing.

With the advent of modern communication systems the distance between two places is measured in kilobytes not kilometers. This has made possible the use of outsourcing for all sizes of companies, whereas before collaboration between design and product development teams located in different parts of the world were limited to major Fortune 500 companies. This excellent way of saving overhead expenses that are in many categories non-productive expenditures, is a major tool available if it fits in any turnaround programme.

The "way forward", now the official name of the Ford Motor Turnaround Programme, for most turnaround companies is not to be just lean and mean, but also flexible. This option was taken by a rising number of companies in recent years, and not just for low cost manufacturing, but for product design and development as well. There have been many occasions where the transferring of the product or need for new product to fresher minds has produced what the company direly needed, and was somehow unable to break the ice at home to do it. Examples of outsourcing are rising by a considerable percentage each year. Examples of outsourcing are companies like Dell Computers and Nike. They no longer are burdened by the high overhead of manufacturing facilities. They have the power of flexibility by outsourcing all they need to manufacture. IKEA is another company among the many. The key to successful outsourcing is akin to making a joint venture work: collaboration on a scale that there are no gaps in goals and objectives between the company and the sourcing manufacturer. In recent years this outsourcing has moved from non-core product manufacturing in a low cost country to core product manufacturing in a low cost country and even to product design and development of core products for a high cost country.
Dell and Nike's operations do away with the traditional supply chain network and can be very flexible in changing the design and amount of component parts and product in order to meet customer needs. They do no t end up with burdensome inventory, stocks, and factory overhead.

However, recent articles have indicated that there may be a danger of outsourcing the high value core products. And companies which do so tend to lose the control or drive to develop their designs and products further at home. The sub-contractors of Dell dream to become Dell one day and may become a competitor.

This is why for example, Nike retains the design and manufacture of the soles of their shoes in their home country of the US, outsourcing the balance of their core product offshore. The subject of outsourcing is a political topic in certain industrial countries as the US. It is likely that certain legislation is in the future to limit the amount of outsourcing. Certain top economists are urging that a free market is not a fair market and the government must enter the transaction in order to balance the loss of jobs that outsourcing can cause with the welfare of its working citizens.

Traditionally in the US, the government has stayed out of the area of trade balance under the ideology that a country should do what it can do best and remain competitive and outsource what another country can do either better or at a lower cost. It is believed that the free system will work out in the end, helping both newly developed countries and developed countries.

This is not uncharted waters to sail in. Germany and Japan in the 1980s faced high valued currencies at home and their products became non-price competitive. Both were forced to find an alternative to stay in the game and continue being manufacturing leaders. They saved the day by outsourcing to SE Asia and to other low cost countries for the manufacture of their products. Today, products from both countries remain very competitive in the world market because they have a balance of plants around the world and have flexibility as one of the tools in their operational kit. It is in many cases important not to be tied down to your in-house resources.

7. "Knowing when to play and when to fold."

Kenny Rogers, a US pop singer, lead the pack of musicians in the eighties with this popular song that has a message for companies in trouble. And the question it infers is not easy to answer. Out of community loyalty, responsibility to the employees and stockholders a company may be reluctant to close a plant that is high cost and no longer competitive. The motivation is commendable, but it may be short term, and in the long run give the employees a false sense of security and the shareholders the same; and unless a decisive move is made their 50% of what they thought they had will turn into closer to 0%.

An example is a company that sustained several manufacturing plants in Wales, a high cost manufacturing climate with strong and contentious labour forces. When it was purchased by a Malaysian company, the Malaysian company wisely closed these high cost plants.

Then came the social problems of unemployment and the reality of low returns on the investments. In this regard, the positions that government must step in with realistic support programs for those affected by forces over which they have little control are probably the answer.

Knowing when to exit and not become a victim of the living dead is a tough decision. The characteristic of being stubborn has its merits. But the flip side of being stubborn is often being stupid, and it is often not easy see where the line between the two breaks. There are sick companies that cannot be brought back to life. This is one of the first points a turnaround expert must answer: Is there a factual and objective basis for a turnaround success?

Within the corporate world, there are the living dead, which are the sick company operating on a wretched existence, without any hope of turnaround. These companies need a miracle such as resurrection from the dead. Many of these companies need a change in DNA or business models. They are technically commercially insolvent and the owners will face the fate of bankruptcy if they close down the operations. Therefore, these dead just hang around, waiting for the death sentence. For some, the death sentence may take years before the owners decide not to throw in good money anymore to chase after bad money. For others, the bubble keeps getting bigger such as the construction companies in Singapore that continue to clinch loss-making projects to cover up for earlier losses in the 1990s.

Banks, too, have cornered themselves into throwing in more loans after the red light has lighted simply because they debt load is so great they are in danger of going down with the debtor. In the eighties the Donald Trump Empire in the US faced such a dilemma and their banks with it. He owed the banks a lot of money then and the banks were unable to press the trigger to stop the flow of credit as they would be dragged down with him.

At time such as the above, when companies are trapped in such situations, the owners have to take some tough decisions to get out of this quandary. It is important to know when to exit. An optimized exit of getting out of non-core or under performing businesses, where there is a loss of confidence in the management and further losses and declining profitability are expected is crucial.

It should be strategic not motivated by panic.

If you are to optimize your exit, then it is no longer perceived as an organization failure but rather an unlocking of your values. Optimized exits should be made strategically. This is because when it is done out of desperation, quite often the value of the company is diminished more than it need be. Successful exits require a lot of good planning for they can maximize shareholder value, minimize costs, liability and disruption, as well as enhance the value of the enterprise.

An optimized exit is necessary for many living dead companies. For some it may mean clearing the deck of the ship prior to an acquisition or integrating a large acquisition that included no unprofitable assets. For others, the business model needs to be revamped with major changes.

There are various ways to bail the company out. One way is to sell the business as an ongoing concern. Another way is to attempt to turn around the company from financial losses before disposal. If the company has a grim chance of turning around, it is best to close the company immediately, cut the losses and move on. There is nothing to be ashamed about with your company going bust. Many successful enterprises suffered failures. This principle is very critical, especially in certain Asian and other countries where a failure is thought to be grounds for losing face, even leading to sickness and death for those responsible or not. One of the greatest religious principles of mankind is the tenet of forgiveness and fresh starts.

Summary of Part IV.

As is shown in Parts III and IV in the more detailed examples of companies there is great impact on companies today by their country and global environment. This, of course, is part of the mosaic of the turnaround process. And this is true without even considering rogue disorder that itself threatens corporate health, and is a deadly corporate virus to any company or country. In a global environment, whether a company participates in international trade or not, this seemingly unstoppable and possibly uncontrollable globalization will affect them in one way or the other.

In the future, the concepts and essentials of turnaround management set forth herein will be one of the most needed business tools of the next decade as China, India and Russia begin the enormous turnaround process of privatizing their struggling state enterprises.

In the west as well, there has to be a better way than going bankrupt as part of the turnaround strategy. The west needs more experienced turnaround professionals not more bankruptcy judges. Today, in the west, it is like the autopsy comes first and the healers and physicians second. And to keep healthy companies healthy many of the turnaround principles and essentials and tool discussed herein are also

applicable. It is hoped this book, *Corporate Turnaround: A Global Perspective*

will aid in the support and success of such companies.

www.ingramcontent.com/pod-product-compliance
Lightning Source LLC
Chambersburg PA
CBHW070527200326
41519CB00013B/2961